Hope When Life's Hard

A 40-Day Devotional to Restore Hope in Your Suffering

Desiree Swift

ETERNAL HOPE
Publishing

HOPE WHEN LIFE'S HARD

Copyright © 2024 by Desiree Swift

All rights reserved.

No portion of this book may be reproduced in any form without written permission from the publisher or author, except as permitted by U.S. copyright law. For permission requests, contact Eternal Hope Ministries at contact@desireeswift.com

ISBN: 979-8-9921435-7-7

All scriptures in this devotional are taken from the New International Version (NIV), unless otherwise noted next to the scripture. Scripture quotations with no designation by them are taken from THE HOLY BIBLE, NEW INTERNATIONAL VERSION®, NIV® Copyright © 1973, 1978, 1984, 2011 by Biblica, Inc.® Used by permission. All rights reserved worldwide.

Scripture quotations marked NLT are taken from the Holy Bible, New Living Translation, copyright © 1996, 2004, 2015 by Tyndale House Foundation. Used by permission of Tyndale House Publishers, Inc., Carol Stream, Illinois 60188. All rights reserved.

Scripture quotations marked (CSB) have been taken from the Christian Standard Bible®, Copyright © 2017 by Holman Bible Publishers. Used by permission. Christian Standard Bible® and CSB® are federally registered trademarks of Holman Bible Publishers.

First edition 2024

Published by Eternal Hope Ministries
www.desireesswift.com

I dedicate this work first to the Lord to use for his glory. Secondly, I dedicate this book to my family who have always been there to get me through the hard times.

ACKNOWLEDGMENTS

To Marilyn Martino, my writing collaborator: This book began because of your simple message. Thank you for your encouragement and partnership.

To Lisa Pierini, my dear friend and mentor: Your guidance over the years has been invaluable. Thank you for sharing your wisdom and asking deep, thought-provoking questions.

To Diana Berns, my uber-creative friend and designer: Your insight into all things publishing was instrumental. Thank you for your guidance.

To my Wednesday Bible study ladies: Our weekly gatherings are a source of strength. Thank you for studying God's Word with me and sharing life.

To my loving in-laws, Cheryl and Vic Swift: Your unwavering support and faithful prayers mean more than I can express. Thank you for always being there.

To my steadfast and amazing parents, Rose and Bob Smith: You have walked with me through every trial and have remained two of my greatest sources of strength. Thank you for your unconditional love and support.

To my awesome kids, Zoey and Jordan Swift: Thank you for your bravery in letting me share your stories, for making me a better person, and for being the wonderful individuals God created you to be. You are the light and joy of my life.

To my incredible husband and man of God, Chris Swift: You are my rock when I'm weak, my clarity when I'm overwhelmed, my haven when I'm weary, and the love of my life. Thank you for your support and for being a blessing beyond measure.

CONTENTS

Before You Begin	xi
How to Use This Devotional	xv
Why a 40-Day Devotional and Not a 30-Day?	xvii
SECTION 1: SUFFERING	1
Day 1 – The Purpose of Suffering	4
Day 2 – Protected Through Suffering	6
Day 3 – Your Suffering Will End	8
Day 4 – No More Suffering, Ever	10
Day 5 – Known and Safe	12
Day 6 – A Constant Comfort	14
Day 7 – Refined by Fire	16
Reflection and Life Application	18
SECTION 2: PEACE IN THE STORM	21
Day 8 – You Are an Overcomer	24
Day 9 – Put Down Your Heavy Load and Rest	26
Day 10 – Guardrails of Peace	28
Day 11 – Waiting When Life is Uncertain	30
Day 12 – Peace in the Stillness	32
Day 13 – Limitless With the Lord	34
Reflection and Life Application	36
SECTION 3: FIXING YOUR EYES ON JESUS	39
Day 14 – Trusting God Without Understanding	42
Day 15 – Unshakable!	44
Day 16 – Press Pause on Worry	46
Day 17 – Laser Focused	48

Cont. SECTION 3: FIXING YOUR EYES ON JESUS

Day 18 – The Power of Praise	50
Day 19 – Worship Over Worry	52
Day 20 – Hide and Seek	54
Reflection and Life Application	56
SECTION 4: GRASPING GOD'S SOVEREIGNTY	59
Day 21 – A Comforting Promise	62
Day 22 – Strength in Weakness	64
Day 23 – Become Like the Son	66
Day 24 – Even If...	68
Day 25 – On a Hospital Floor	70
Day 26 – In the Potter's Hands	72
Day 27 – Not Because of My Sin	74
Reflection and Life Application	76
SECTION 5: FAITH OVER FEAR	79
Day 28 – Free From Fear	82
Day 29 – How to Stop Your Racing Thoughts	84
Day 30 – A Simple Mental Checklist	86
Day 31 – Fear Not, the Battle Belongs to the Lord	88
Day 32 – Standing on Solid Ground	90
Day 33 – Be Strong and Courageous	92
Reflection and Life Application	94
SECTION 6: HOPE WHEN LIFE'S HARD	97
Day 34 – Rooted Deeply in Living Water	100
Day 35 – Hope From Suffering	102
Day 36 – The Promise of a New Body	104

Cont. SECTION 6: HOPE WHEN LIFE'S HARD

Day 37 – Overflowing With Hope	106
Day 38 – Resting on True Hope	108
Day 39 – Plans of Hope and a Future	110
Day 40 – Heard and Rescued	112
Reflection and Life Application	114
About the Author	117
An Invitation from the Author	119

BEFORE YOU BEGIN

Suffering is an undeniable reality we all face in this life—a universal human experience born of living in a fallen and broken world. For some, it wrecks them; for others, it strengthens and refines them. What determines whether we thrive through suffering or merely survive it? I believe the answer lies in where we fix our eyes during the trials.

Nobody wants to call themselves an expert in suffering, but I will say that I have faced my fair share, as I'm sure you have too. I write this as a cancer mom. My 13-year-old son is battling his second fight with cancer and is currently undergoing chemotherapy. He has a rare condition called Langerhans Cell Histiocytosis, which causes rapidly growing tumors that eat through his bones. One tumor required brain surgery, while the second was too risky to operate on, necessitating a year-long chemotherapy regimen.

Beyond this, to name just a few of my struggles, I have endured the devastation of a failing marriage (thankfully redeemed by God), walked alongside a child struggling with mental health issues due to her brother's cancer (whom God has rescued and strengthened), and wrestled with over thirty years of a debilitating personal battle with anxiety and fear (from which God has set me free).

Our family experienced the heartbreak of a cherished friendship collapsing, the brokenness, loss, and rejection shocked us deeply (a wound still healing). And I currently live with chronic, severe back pain and limited mobility caused by fractured and slipped vertebrae, pinched nerves, and torn discs (which God has not yet healed).

I share these trials not to prove anything but to walk alongside you. If you are reading this book, I assume you too have faced suffering or are in the midst of a hard trial, seeking encouragement. The scriptures I've chosen for this devotional are some of my most treasured ones—verses that have carried me through seasons of suffering.

I pray they will do the same for you. May each devotion bring meaning to your suffering, provide comfort, peace, encouragement, and hope, and help you keep your eyes focused on God. My stories may not change your life, but God's promises will.

I write this devotional from the heart of the storm of childhood cancer and chronic pain—not from the calm after it. I am walking through the fire with you. These are tried-and-true practices and scriptures that are sustaining me in my pain, and I pray they will meet you in yours.

Although I do not believe all suffering is caused by God, I know he uses it all for good. One profound lesson I have learned through suffering is this: God always has a purpose for it. He does not allow his children to suffer without reason. Instead, he uses our pain as a tool to refine, strengthen, and equip us for his purposes. His plan for our suffering is for good. Knowing his sovereignty over my pain brings me peace, hope, and even joy. I pray this truth will bring the same to your heart.

I leave you with four simple words that I hope will anchor you. These four words were spoken to me by a friend in the depth of some of my suffering and brought me peace when everything felt hopeless: "Everything will be OK." This is not a hollow platitude meant to dismiss your pain, but a reassurance rooted in God's promises. It's an eternal forecast of the good things to come.

I know your current suffering may seem unbearable and impossible. And four words like those above may feel heartless. But the goal is to get your eyes fixed on the eternal promises of God, when everything really will be ok. Everything in this life may never feel ok, but we have an eternity of perfection promised to us by a God that never lets us down. He sees you. He hears you. He has a plan for your suffering. He will be your strength, provide for your every need, and never leave you alone.

With prayers and blessings,

Desiree Swift

HOW TO USE THIS DEVOTIONAL

This devotional contains 40 entries. You can choose to read them chronologically over the next 40 days or select the ones that resonate most with your current season of life. If you choose not to read them chronologically, I encourage you to pray before each reading, asking God to guide you to the entry that speaks to your heart.

Before beginning your daily devotion, take a moment to pause and invite God to reveal something new to you—whether through the devotion itself or directly from his Word. I also encourage you to have a physical Bible on hand. Looking up the scripture in your Bible allows you to read the surrounding verses, and God often speaks powerfully through the context of his Word.

To help you navigate the devotional, I've categorized the entries into the following six topics: 1. Suffering, 2. Peace in the Storm, 3. Fixing Your Eyes on Jesus, 4. Grasping God's Sovereignty, 5. Faith Over Fear, and 6. Hope When Life's Hard. These topics flow naturally in this order, but feel free to read them as you feel led.

At the end of each topic, you'll find a brief Reflection and Life Application section. I strongly encourage you to take the time to complete these exercises. Reading is powerful, but true transformation happens when we reflect on and apply what we've learned. To take it a step further, consider highlighting a few meaningful verses, memorizing them, and asking God to help you live them out in your daily life.

Having scripture memorized equips us to apply God's truth even in the most difficult moments. When I'm overwhelmed and crying on my bed, it's much harder to get up, find my Bible, and read than it is to speak a scripture aloud from memory.

Many of the scriptures in this book are ones I've memorized because I've leaned on them countless times during my suffering. Every time I recite them, they remind me of God's goodness, power, faithfulness, and promises. They bring peace, joy, and hope—reassuring me that everything will ultimately be okay because God is good and sovereign over all.

WHY A 40-DAY DEVOTIONAL AND NOT A 30-DAY?

When I first began writing this devotional, my plan was to stop at 30 entries. However, as I completed the 30th devotion, I felt a clear prompting from God to keep going to 40. At the time, I didn't understand why. But as I began researching the significance of the number 40 in the Bible, I became even more amazed by God's plans.

The number 40 holds incredible meaning throughout scripture. It is often associated with periods of testing, trial, and transformation, as well as the fulfillment of God's promises. Many biblical scholars believe that the number 40 signifies growth, renewal, and new beginnings.

Here are just a few examples of significant events in the Bible that lasted 40 days:

- Jesus fasted and was tempted in the wilderness for 40 days and nights before beginning his ministry. (Matthew 4:2; Luke 4:2; Mark 1:13)
- Noah's family endured 40 days and nights of rain during the flood that covered the earth, preserving only those on the ark. (Genesis 7:4)
- Goliath taunted the Israelites for 40 days before David, through God's strength, defeated him. (1 Samuel 17:16)

- Moses fasted for 40 days on Mount Sinai as he sought God and received the law. (Exodus 24:18; 34:28)
- Jesus remained on earth for 40 days after his resurrection to teach and prepare his disciples before ascending to heaven. (Acts 1:3)

As I studied these examples, I realized how perfectly the number 40 aligns with the theme of this devotional: finding hope in suffering and trials. The Bible often connects the number 40 with enduring hardships, trusting God's promises, and experiencing transformation. How fitting that this devotional should span 40 days, encouraging us to lean into God's faithfulness during our own seasons of trial.

My prayer is that over these 40 days, you will experience renewal and transformation through the power of God's promises. I pray that he will:

- Transform your fear into faith,
- Replace your hopelessness with his peace,
- Help you grasp his sovereignty,
- Turn your worry into worship, and
- Refocus your eyes on him.

Let's embark on this journey together, trusting that God is working through our trials to fulfill his promises.

Let's get started!

Section 1

Reflections and Daily Devotions on Suffering

SUFFERING

Suffering is hard. Nobody wants to suffer. Yet, it is an undeniable part of the human experience. Whether we call it a trial, challenge, struggle, hard time, or valley, we all face moments of deep pain and difficulty.

My goal in this devotional is to help reframe suffering through a biblical lens, allowing us to see it as something purposeful and fruitful—not something to dread or wallow in. I know this perspective may sound counterintuitive, even crazy. But stay with me.

It's not about being excited for suffering but about reaching a place where we can endure it with peace, trusting that God is with us in the midst of it. Where we grow closer to him and cling to His goodness, even when life feels anything but good. Why? Because suffering, when viewed through God's promises, has a higher purpose, and he will use it for good.

God is sovereign. He created all, knows all, sees all, and controls all. His sovereignty means that your suffering is not random or meaningless. He has allowed it for a reason. He trusts you with this trial, knowing that you can use it to reflect his glory to others and deepen your faith. And God knows you will grow through the suffering.

It's important to note that not all suffering is the same. There is a distinction between suffering that results from our own sin and suffering that lies entirely outside of our control. If you are experiencing suffering and have already repented of any sin and sought God in prayer to remove it, yet the trial remains, take heart. You can rest assured that God has a purpose for allowing it. He is working in ways that may not yet be visible.

Let's explore together what the Bible says about suffering. Scripture offers profound insight, comfort, and hope for these difficult seasons!

> ***PRAYER****: Lord, please help me see suffering and trials through your eyes. I pray for your strength, hope, love, joy, and peace to be with me in my trials. Please give me opportunities to use my experiences of suffering to help others. In Jesus' name, amen.*

Day 1
The Purpose of Suffering

In all this you greatly rejoice, though now for a little while you may have had to suffer grief in all kinds of trials. These have come so that the proven genuineness of your faith—of greater worth than gold, which perishes even though refined by fire—may result in praise, glory and honor when Jesus Christ is revealed. —1 PETER 1:6-7

During one morning quiet time, after receiving the devastating news that our son's cancer had returned, I found myself pleading with the Lord, asking why this was happening again. We had believed he was healed the first time. In response, I felt prompted to read 1 Peter chapter 1. Just six verses in, I found an incredible answer from the Lord. In today's two short verses, he gave me peace and clarity, showing me that this second diagnosis was a test of the genuineness of our faith—a way to refine it. The result, he revealed, would be praise, glory, and honor.

Would I have ever chosen childhood cancer for our son to achieve these things from the Lord? Absolutely not. Yet here we were, facing this trial once more—this time not brain surgery, but a year of chemotherapy.

Though I wished our circumstances could be different, God's response through Scripture brought me a deep sense of peace. It assured me that our family's suffering was not meaningless. I was comforted to know that the Lord had heard my cries and had chosen to answer me. In the midst of it all, I realized I was not alone in my suffering. He was right there with me.

Your suffering has a purpose too. The Lord allows it to test and refine the genuineness of your faith. Through it, he is preparing a reward of praise, glory, and honor when Christ returns. And most importantly, you are never alone. God sees you, he hears your cries, and he has a plan for you.

I understand this may be a difficult message to accept, especially when you're in the midst of pain. Yet, we must remember that God's ultimate goal is to refine us into the likeness of Christ. Suffering is one of the most powerful tools he uses to shape us into the character of his Son.

> ***PRAYER****: Lord, please help me feel peace in the message that my suffering has a purpose. Thank you that I am not just pointlessly facing these trials and that you have allowed them and are overseeing them. In Jesus' name, amen.*

Day 2
Protected Through Suffering

We are pressed on every side by troubles, but we are not crushed. We are perplexed, but not driven to despair. We are hunted down, but never abandoned by God. We get knocked down, but we are not destroyed. Through suffering, our bodies continue to share in the death of Jesus so that the life of Jesus may also be seen in our bodies.
—2 CORINTHIANS 4:8-10

One household chore our son truly enjoys is crushing cans. We have an old can crusher mounted on our garage wall, and he loves placing a can in it, pressing down hard on the handle, and then hearing that final CRACK as the can flattens. That crushed can is the image that comes to mind when I read this verse.

There have been moments in my suffering where I tangibly feel like an invisible force is pressing down on me from every side—just like that can crusher. Yet, I can honestly say that despite the intense pressure, I have never been crushed.

This verse also mentions feeling perplexed. Oh, I can absolutely relate to that! Most of the time, I don't understand how God is working. My limited, human mind struggles to comprehend his infinite ways. And yet, even in my confusion, I have not been driven to despair.

The passage also speaks of being knocked down but not destroyed. Praise God for that promise! I know what it feels like to be shaken or knocked down, but by relying on the Lord's strength, I've been able to stand back up and keep moving forward.

Can you relate to feeling pressed on every side, perplexed by troubles, hunted down, or knocked down? I imagine you can. But can you also see God's goodness in the fact that you have not been crushed, abandoned by God, or destroyed?

Even when it doesn't feel like it, God is protecting you through your suffering. Picture something jamming the enemy's can crusher just as he tries to destroy you. You might get a little crumpled or bent out of shape, but you're not crushed beyond repair. That is God's protection at work because he loves you and has a purpose for your suffering. One purpose this verse highlights is reflecting the life of Jesus through our trials!

> **PRAYER**: *Lord, thank you for protecting me in my suffering. Thank you that I am not crushed, led to despair, or abandoned by you. Please help me reflect the life of Jesus through my suffering and bring you glory. In Jesus' name, amen.*

Day 3

Your Suffering Will End

And the God of all grace, who called you to his eternal glory in Christ, after you have suffered a little while, will himself restore you and make you strong, firm, and steadfast. — 1 PETER 5:10

In July 2023, my dad and I participated in a bike ride called The Agony. This 24-hour endurance ride raises funds to shepherd young adults toward healing in Christ. Hundreds of cyclists battle high winds, rough roads, extreme temperatures, sleep deprivation, and more—all to support these young adults and introduce them to the love of Jesus. By the end of the 24 hours, my dad and I had each clocked in 228 miles.

You could say we suffered on numerous levels. But two things kept us motivated: knowing the suffering had an end and knowing it had a purpose. We knew that after 24 hours, we'd get off our bikes and rest—no more saddle sores, no more numb feet, and no more nausea from dehydration. And most importantly, the funds raised would help young adults grow in their discipleship program.

Today's verse brings me so much peace in my trials and suffering because it reminds me there is an end. The suffering during The Agony ride was nothing compared to the two-and-a-half years (and counting) of my son's cancer battle. But I hold onto the truth that his battle will have an end. One day, he will finish chemotherapy, stop undergoing surgeries and scans, and experience relief from the chemotherapy side effects. Someday, God willing, he'll return to a normal life.

This verse promises that our suffering will last only "a little while." We must remember that God sees time differently than we do. The Bible describes our entire lives as a "vapor"—barely a blip in the grand history of time. So, even a multi-year battle with cancer is considered "a little while" in the context of eternity.

Another beautiful promise in this verse is that after our suffering, God will restore us and make us strong, firm, and steadfast. After your short season of suffering, God will restore you too! I am so looking forward to that time!

> **PRAYER**: *Dear Father, thank you so much that my suffering is temporary. Thank you for being so good at restoring and strengthening me after my suffering has ended. Please help me live in gratitude for these great promises. In Jesus' name, amen.*

Day 4
No More Suffering, Ever

He will wipe every tear from their eyes, and there will be no more death, or sorrow, or crying, or pain. All these things are gone forever. — REVELATION 21:4 (NLT)

When I am in the thick of suffering, I desperately need solid promises to focus on, and this verse is one of them. Today's reading amplifies the promise we reflected on yesterday. Yesterday, we were reminded that our seasons of suffering are short and will come to an end. But today's verse assures us that all our suffering will eventually end—forever.

I recall a time not too long ago when it felt like every area of my life was being tested. Our son had a second cancerous tumor and was beginning chemo. At the same time, our daughter was battling depression and anxiety due to her brother's cancer, a close friendship had shattered, my husband was enduring a significant trial at work, and I was in agonizing back pain with limited mobility. It was a true whirlwind of trials and suffering. Any one of those challenges would have been difficult to face alone, but I was carrying all of them at once.

The promise in today's verse was pivotal in helping me persevere. The assurance that one day there will be no more suffering brought calm and God's peace into my storm. During that season, I faced everything this verse describes—grief from a broken relationship, sorrow over my son's health, crying from heartbreak, and the relentless pain of my own physical condition. Yet, this verse reminds us of an eternity where none of those terrible things exist. I can only imagine how glorious that will be!

In difficult times, I often say, "I don't know how people endure suffering without God." Without his promises, how do they find hope or strength to keep going? In my journey of suffering, I've frequently thought or whispered to myself, "It will all eventually be over. This won't last forever." These simple declarations of God's promises have calmed my heart and brought peace. They remind me of God's goodness and strengthen me to face another day, another challenge.

Your suffering will end too. I'm not just saying your current trial will pass, only to be replaced by more suffering. I mean all your trials and pain will end forever. Every tear, every hurt, every stress, every sorrow—it will all end. Forever. Cling to that promise!

> **PRAYER**: *Father, thank you for today's promise that all my suffering will end. Please help me remember this promise in times of suffering and help me persevere through. In Jesus' name, amen.*

Day 5
Known and Safe

Do not be afraid, for I have ransomed you. I have called you by name; you are mine. When you go through deep waters, I will be with you. When you go through rivers of difficulty, you will not drown. When you walk through the fire of oppression, you will not be burned up; the flames will not consume you. For I am the Lord, your God,... —ISAIAH 43:1b-3a (NLT)

This verse reminds me of a time I was snorkeling in the ocean. My husband and I had ventured beyond the coral reef and found ourselves in the endless expanse of the vast Pacific Ocean. The tide was coming in, and the waters were tumultuous. I looked around but couldn't see my husband. I was sure that he, too, was battling the waves.

Fear began to creep in as I struggled in the raging waters of the incoming tide. I was trying to avoid being smashed into the hard coral while fighting to keep my head above water. This battle lasted for about 20 minutes as we made our way toward a distant beach. I was in deep water, felt utterly alone, and faced the terrifying possibility of drowning. In that moment, I would have given anything to feel safe and to have someone by my side to help.

There have been many times when I've felt emotionally overwhelmed, as if I were drowning in the crashing waves of suffering. I'm sure you have, too. I would also describe much of my suffering as being in the fire, just as this verse mentions—those hard moments when I don't feel seen, known, or safe.

Oh, how we long to be known and to feel safe. These are two of the deepest human needs. This verse brings us the beautiful promises of God: not only does he know us personally, but he will keep us safe in our struggles and trials. When we are emotionally drowning or caught in the fires of life, he is with us, protecting us.

What this verse also promises is that we will go through hard times. It says, "When you go...." and "When you walk...," not if you go through or walk through. A struggle for many Christians is the false belief that they shouldn't face hardships in life. The Bible clearly tells us otherwise. But we can maintain hope through these struggles, knowing that the God of the universe, who redeemed us and knows us, will keep us safe.

***PRAYER**: Father God, thank you so much for the promises that you know me and will keep me safe in my trials and suffering. Please help me be unafraid as I face and go through hard times. In Jesus' name, amen.*

Day 6

A Constant Comfort

He comforts us in all our troubles so that we can comfort others. When they are troubled, we will be able to give them the same comfort God has given us.
—2 CORINTHIANS 1:3-4 (NLT)

God has used many of my hardest trials to bring comfort to others. You can read more about some of them in the "Before You Begin" section at the beginning of this book if you haven't already. Each one of those trials hurt deeply and some leave lingering pain. Yet, God has restored and redeemed many of them, and we continue to pray for those still unresolved.

Through it all, I've used those painful experiences to help others who are navigating similar struggles. God has transformed my suffering into light and hope for those walking through their own darkness.

In the midst of my suffering, I cried out to God, and he brought me comfort. Now, I have the privilege of sharing that comfort with others. I sit with them in their tears, walking alongside them through extreme loss, broken relationships, failing marriages, chronic pain, and the health struggles of their children.

What a beautiful plan God has for suffering: to equip us to be comforters to those in the miry pits.

God's purpose for our trials—to bring comfort to others—infuses meaning into even the hardest experiences we endure. While we may not always be able to help others during the worst of our struggles, we can rely on the Holy Spirit to empower us to serve others once we've emerged from the depths.

There is great power, joy, and fulfillment in bringing comfort to someone in need, especially when our personal experiences allow us to illuminate their darkness. However, it requires intention, a willingness to share our stories, and the courage to bring hope. Do not hide your suffering or push it under a rug, denying it the chance to comfort someone else. Your story and experience could be the very testimony that brings someone hope and peace!

> ***PRAYER***: *Good Father, thank you for having many purposes and plans for my suffering. Thank you that one of those plans is for me to bring comfort to others who are hurting. Please embolden me to share my story and struggles to help others. In Jesus' name, amen.*

Day 7
Refined by Fire

Dear friends, don't be surprised at the fiery trials you are going through, as if something strange were happening to you. Instead, be very glad—for these trials make you partners with Christ in his suffering, so that you will have the wonderful joy of seeing his glory when it is revealed to all the world. —1 PETER 4:12-13 (NLT)

Experienced silversmiths understand that placing silver in the fire is essential for refining and purifying it. As the silver melts, the silversmith carefully observes it, knowing precisely how much time it needs in the heat. When the silversmith can see their reflection in the molten silver, they know the refining process is complete.

God uses fiery trials in much the same way for us. He knows how hardships and suffering can refine us and purify our faith. In our family's experiences, when the heat of trial intensifies, we've found ourselves drawing closer to him. These moments create opportunities for God to refine and purify us.

God's ultimate goal for his children is to shape us into the image of Jesus, so that we reflect his likeness to the world. Just as the silversmith watches over the silver in the fire, God allows us time in the fire to refine us until we reflect his image.

This truth became especially meaningful to me when we discovered that my son's cancer had returned. At first, the situation felt surreal and overwhelming. During prayer, God brought today's verse to my attention that profoundly shifted my perspective. The verse reminded me not to consider my son's cancer as strange and taught me that our family's suffering was a way to share in Christ's sufferings, ultimately leading to a promise of great joy when his glory is revealed. Those powerful promises gave me strength and hope.

Although enduring the trials of childhood cancer and subsequent teenage depression has been incredibly challenging, we have sought—with God's help—to reflect his hope, truth, love, peace, and strength to the world.

God is also refining you in the fire as his precious silver, with the goal of seeing his reflection. Your suffering is in the hands of the Master Crafter. He's watching closely and knows what he's doing.

PRAYER*: Lord, thank you for watching over my life and for being in control. Help me not to see my suffering as strange, but to find joy in it, knowing it partners me with Jesus. Please guide me to reflect your image to the world. In Jesus' name, amen.*

Reflection and Life Application

1) What verse from this section was most meaningful to me? *(Write it out here)* _____
_____
_____
_____
_____

2) What did I learn about suffering that I didn't know? Or what was I reminded of that I already knew? _____
_____
_____
_____
_____

3) What from this section on suffering encouraged me and brought me hope? _____
_____
_____
_____
_____

4) How has my perspective on suffering changed since reading through this section? _____
_____
_____
_____
_____

5) What am I suffering through right now that I can trust God to use for good? _____

_____
_____
_____
_____

6) Any other thoughts or takeaways about suffering? _____

_____
_____
_____
_____
_____
_____

***PRAYER**: Heavenly Father, thank you for your promises and truths about suffering. Please help me take what you've shown me through this section on suffering and apply it to my life. Help me have a better perspective on suffering, that you have a plan for all my trials and troubles, and you are using them for my good. In Jesus' name, amen.*

Section 2

Reflections and Daily Devotions for Having Peace in the Storm

PEACE IN THE STORM

Peace. Just the word itself brings a sense of calm to me now. We deeply desire peace, and I am so grateful that Jesus enables us to experience peace even during life's hardest moments. That is one of the profound miracles of our Christian faith.

For many people, peace seems to be the opposite of suffering. They believe that you either suffer and lose peace, or avoid suffering and find peace. But that's not true. One of the miracles and blessings of our faith is that we can experience peace, hope, joy, and love—even in the darkest times. It sounds radical and unlikely, but it's true!

When our son needed brain surgery to remove a rapidly growing tumor, and during the long year of his chemotherapy, I experienced a tangible peace and joy. I wasn't consumed by worry or anxiety. That kind of peace is only possible with God.

What I've learned, however, is that having peace in the midst of trials is not the default human response. Fear, worry, stress, anxiety, anger, despair, and hopelessness are natural reactions to difficult situations. To have peace, we must be intentional in seeking God and relying on him for his perfect peace.

Every night, I pray over my children, asking God to fill and cover them with his perfect shalom. Shalom, the Hebrew word for peace, carries a meaning far deeper than our English understanding. It signifies wholeness, completeness, and a state of total well-being—perfect peace and wellness.

I pray these same words over you, that God will fill and cover you with his perfect shalom. I pray that you will experience his peace even when facing pain, sorrow, and troubles of many kinds. Because of Jesus, you have access to the miracle of peace in the storm. He may not always calm the storm, but he will calm his child in the storm.

PRAYER: *Dear Lord, thank you for your perfect peace, your shalom. Please help me keep my eyes fixed on you in my suffering so I can experience your peace, joy, hope, and love in my hardest times. I ask for your perfect shalom to fill me and cover me as I journey through my suffering. In Jesus' name, amen.*

Day 8

You Are an Overcomer

I have told you these things, so that in me you may have peace. In this world you will have trouble. But take heart! I have overcome the world. —JOHN 16:33

These are some of Jesus' most comforting words. He was speaking to his disciples about his upcoming departure—a moment that must have been daunting for them. Imagine being one of those disciples: the man we were following, our Lord, Master, and Teacher, was telling us he was going to leave. How could we possibly continue without him? What if we faced troubles or struggles in ministering without his physical presence?

Jesus' words were meant to bring peace to his disciples in that moment, and they continue to bring us peace today in our own trials. Yes, he acknowledges that we will face struggles, but he also reassures us that he has already overcome all the troubles in the world!

With this proclamation of victory, Jesus invites us to focus on triumph instead of the appearance of defeat we often see in hard times. Jesus, the King of kings, the Lord of lords, the name above all names—before whom every knee will bow—has already conquered every struggle and trouble this world can bring. This truth should fill us with awe for God's sovereignty and his unmatched power over all our trials.

Nothing can defeat us because he has already conquered our enemies and overcome every hardship. We are overcomers because Jesus is THE Overcomer. In my own seasons of suffering, I have often clung to this verse, and it has blanketed me with Jesus' peace.

Take a moment to read this verse again, truly believe it, and let it settle in your heart. You can have peace in this world, even in the midst of your struggles, because Jesus has overcome them all!

> ***PRAYER***: *Lord Jesus, thank you so much for the truth of your peace. Thank you that as a child of God, I can have peace even in my suffering. And thank you that you have overcome the troubles of the world. Please help me to rest in the peace of your victory over my troubles. In your mighty name, amen.*

Day 9
Put Down Your Heavy Load and Rest

Come to me all who are weary and burdened, and I will give you rest. Take my yoke upon you and learn from me, for I am gentle and humble in heart, and you will find rest for your souls. For my yoke is easy and my burden is light.
—MATTHEW 11:28-30

Backpacking is one of my favorite outdoor adventures. I've been backpacking since my teenage years, and it's a passion I still cherish. There's nothing quite like being surrounded by God's glorious creation, carrying everything I need for survival on my back—it's a grand adventure. But it's also a heavy load.

I'm not a super ultralight backpacker, so my gear and food usually weigh about 35 pounds for a four-day trip. That might not sound like much, but when it's strapped to my back and hips for hours on end, mile after mile, it becomes a significant burden.

I'm constantly aware of its presence and weight as I maneuver over rocks, climb steep hills, and descend into deep canyons. But when it's time to remove my pack during a break, the feeling is indescribable. A literal weight is lifted from my shoulders, my muscles relax, and I can take a deep, full breath.

This experience reminds me of the times when God has lifted spiritual and emotional burdens from me. In those moments, I feel as though an actual weight has been removed. I often describe it as feeling lighter, able to breathe more easily, and move freely. It's an incredible gift—a miracle from God—when he takes away my stress, worries, and troubles.

God is such a loving and generous Father, always ready to take our heavy burdens and replace them with his light and manageable one. Today's passage promises that he will lift your burdens too. But there's an essential step: you must willingly remove those burdens and hand them over to him. God won't take them without your willingness to let them go.

PRAYER: *Heavenly Father, thank you for offering to take my heavy load and give me your light burden. I ask you now to please take this heavy load off of me. Please help me walk lighter, breathe easier, and trust you more with my life. In Jesus' name, amen.*

Day 10

Guardrails of Peace

Do not be anxious about anything, but in every situation, by prayer and petition, with thanksgiving, present your requests to God. And the peace of God, which transcends all understanding, will guard your hearts and your minds in Christ Jesus. —PHILIPPIANS 4:6-7

I'm an avid hiker and outdoor adventurer, and one of the most memorable hikes I've done is Half Dome in Yosemite National Park. On the edge of the dome, there's a section where I must climb between two large cables secured to the rock.

These cables guide me and keep me focused on the greater goal of reaching the top. They also protect me from falling down the sheer sides of the massive rock dome—4,000 feet to the valley floor below. Like guardrails, I tightly hold onto them to stay on the right path and safe from danger. Without those cables or climbing gear, it would be impossible to ascend the dome.

Today's verses remind me of those cables—they are my spiritual guardrails. I cling to them to gain God's peace, comfort, and direction, and to refocus when life feels overwhelming. Of all the verses I've memorized, these are the ones I recall, the most.

These verses have carried me through thirty years of debilitating fear and anxiety. They calm my heart and mind when I face the worries and fears of childhood cancer. They guided and comforted me during the heartbreak of a failing marriage. They keep my eyes fixed on the goodness and peace of God, even in the midst of what often feels like an impossible journey.

These scriptures are a powerful reminder that we truly don't need to be anxious about anything, because God is in control of everything. If we could live with this mindset consistently, imagine how much greater and freer our lives would be!

I can honestly say that even in my most troubling and challenging times I've experienced a peace that cannot be explained. A peace that is only possible by clinging to the guardrails of scripture and God's unwavering goodness.

You don't have to be anxious about anything. Anxiety, illogical fear, and worry add no value to your life. God's got you, and he's offering his peace to your heart and mind. If you don't feel it in your current situation, ask him to fill you with his peace.

***PRAYER**: Heavenly Father, thank you for your peace that transcends all understanding. Thank you for guarding my heart and mind even in the hardest of times. Please help me feel your peace in a way only you can do. In Jesus' name, amen.*

Day 11

Waiting When Life Is Uncertain

Peace I leave with you; my peace I give you I do not give as the world gives. Do not let your hearts be troubled and do not be afraid. — JOHN 14:27

This past weekend was one filled with waiting. It had the potential to stir up a lot of fear, and it served as a clear reminder of the new normal we live in. It also highlighted how much we need to rely on God during life's uncertainties and struggles.

For a week, our son had been mentioning worsening pain in his spine whenever he jumped. Normally, a bit of physical discomfort in a growing teenager wouldn't be a reason to contact the doctor. But for us, we can't ignore even small pains because of his history with cancer.

A little pain for Jordan can quickly turn into a bone-eating tumor in two weeks. If not a new tumor, the pain could have been a fracture from the year of steroid treatments for cancer. So, we contacted his doctor, who immediately ordered X-rays. We went on Friday, and then the waiting began.

Typically, we receive results within hours, but this time, there was no news for two days. The waiting was excruciating. Thoughts about what it might mean if this were a new tumor filled our minds. It was especially hard because, as I write this, Jordan is just weeks away from finishing chemotherapy!

Yet, I'm incredibly grateful for how God has transformed my perspective. I wasn't gripped by fear or worry. Both my husband and I agreed: if God allowed another tumor, then he had a purpose for it, and we would keep moving forward.

There is so much freedom and peace in no longer wrestling with fear and worry. Only God can take away such strongholds! Did we want Jordan to have another tumor? Of course not. But would we eventually trust and accept whatever our Lord allowed to happen? Yes, because he is in control, and we are not.

This childhood cancer journey has brought us to a place of deeper trust and greater appreciation for God's sovereignty. There is abundant peace in letting God be God. We will never fully understand how he works, but we can trust that his ways are always good. Thankfully, on Sunday afternoon, we received the results: no new tumor and no fracture!

I share this story to encourage you in your seasons of suffering and waiting. In times of uncertainty, you too can experience peace. You can trust God even in the hardest moments, without being crushed by worry and fear. If you find yourself struggling with fear or worry, ask the Lord to set you free from their grip.

PRAYER: *Father God, thank you for giving me a peace that the world can't give or take away, even in hard times. Please help me focus on and trust you more. In Jesus' name, amen.*

Day 12

Peace in the Stillness

The Lord will fight for you; you need only to be still. — EXODUS 14:14

During an evening Bible study, I shared how utterly exhausted I was from the ongoing battles in my life. For years, I had been warring in prayer, not only for my family but for hundreds of others while also serving in ministry. The exhaustion was emotional, mental, and physical, and I wasn't experiencing the peace of God that I so desperately needed.

Two of my friends in the Bible study receive visions from the Lord, and one of them shared a vision she had as I was describing my exhaustion. With tears in her eyes, she told me she saw me dressed as a warrior, limping off the battlefield with a bloody leg. She described me entering a tent, where I sat in a chair next to Jesus. He was there, tending to my wounds, restoring me, and encouraging me to rest while he took over and fought my battles. My other prophetic friend confirmed the same vision.

This vision reminded me of today's passage, where the Israelites faced what seemed like an impossible battle. Trapped between the uncrossable Red Sea ahead and Pharaoh's military forces charging behind, they were overwhelmed with fear and despair. Yet, Moses, with immense faith and a deep connection to God, told them to be still and let the Lord fight for them.

In their fear, the Israelites struggled to trust God, even after He had miraculously delivered them from slavery in Egypt. But God showed His faithfulness once again. As Moses obeyed and raised his staff, God parted the Red Sea, allowing the Israelites to cross safely. When the Egyptians pursued them, God released the waters, drowning Pharaoh's army and securing victory for his people.

This story is a profound reminder of God's faithfulness, power, and love. He fought their battle, brought them peace, and proved that he is completely worthy of trust.

In my own struggles, this story brings me so much comfort. It reminds me that sometimes, God calls me to be still and let him fight my battles. When we're overwhelmed by spiritual or physical struggles, it's easy to lose sight of his peace. But when we step back and allow him to take over, we can experience the abundant peace that only he provides.

Are you facing an impossible battle that's stealing your peace? Ask God to help you be still and trust him to fight for you.

> **PRAYER**: *Father God, thank you for fighting my battles and encouraging me to just be still and trust you. Please help me be still and trust you because it does not come naturally to me. In Jesus' name, amen.*

Day 13

Limitless With the Lord

I can do all things through Christ who strengthens me. —PHILIPPIANS 4:13

These ten words have carried me through countless challenges, hardships, and seasons of suffering. They've brought renewed peace in the midst of chaos. Whether I was pushing through the demands of an endurance race, walking through the deep darkness of my child's teen depression, navigating the endless unknowns of childhood cancer, enduring the heartbreak of rejection and broken relationships, or persevering through chronic pain from a broken back, this verse has been my solid rock.

Paul originally wrote these words to the church in Philippi to share his perspective on suffering and encourage them in their own trials. He spoke of experiencing both the lowest of lows and the highest of highs and revealed the secret he had learned: to be content in all circumstances. Then, he declared the source of his strength, saying, "I can do all things through Christ who strengthens me."

Imagine how different our lives would be if we truly believed this promise. If we wholeheartedly trusted that we could face anything with Jesus' strength, how much less would we worry? Would we be bolder to take on hard things and follow God's calling? Would we confront our fears, insecurities, and strongholds more confidently?

One thing is certain: if we truly lived by this verse, we would experience more of God's peace. It's impossible to focus on the truth of Jesus' strength and love for us while fixating on worries, fears, and hurts. This verse has helped me overcome trials and achieve what once seemed impossible.

So, I challenge you: memorize these words, speak them aloud, and cling to them in times of need. When you face an impossible situation or a bold assignment, proclaim with faith, "I can do all things through Christ who strengthens me." Say it boldly—not as a rote recitation, but as a declaration of truth and trust in Jesus' power.

> **PRAYER**: *Lord, thank you for always being my strength. Thank you for making the impossible possible. Please help me recall the truth from Philippians 4:13 when faced with something hard. In Jesus' name, amen.*

Reflection and Life Application

1) What verse from this section was most meaningful to me? *(Write it out here)* _____
_____
_____
_____
_____

2) What did I learn about peace that I didn't know before? Or what was I reminded of that I already knew?_____
_____
_____
_____
_____

3) What from this section on peace encouraged me and brought me hope? _____
_____
_____
_____
_____

4) How has my perspective on peace in the storm changed since reading through this section? _____
_____
_____
_____
_____

5) Where do I need God's peace the most right now? _____
_____
_____
_____
_____

6) Any other thoughts or takeaways about peace in the storm? _____
_____
_____
_____
_____
_____
_____
_____
_____

***PRAYER**: Heavenly Father, thank you for your promises and truths about peace. Please help me take what you've shown me through this section on peace and apply it to my life. Help me have peace in my storms and trust you more when life feels hard. In Jesus' name, amen.*

Section 3

Reflections and Daily Devotions for Fixing Your Eyes on Jesus

FIXING YOUR EYES ON JESUS

I used to compete in triathlons. The races included a swim in open water, a bike ride, and a run. To stay on the swim course, I would do a few strokes and then look up to find the big buoys to stay headed in the right direction.

If I got too determined, distracted, or tired, I would forget to look up every few strokes and drift off course. The next time I glanced up, I would struggle to find the buoy and have to work harder to get back on course. This error made my whole race longer and harder.

Keeping our eyes fixed on a target is also important in daily life. When we face a hard or hurtful situation, our natural tendencies are to either try to fix the problem or shut down. We focus on whatever information we can find. By focusing on our circumstances and possible solutions, we take our eyes off our Savior—the One who is the best remedy for our problem.

Our circumstances and the storm around us are the worst places to fix our eyes. These faulty fixations make the situation seem even bigger in our minds and open the door to hopelessness, discouragement, and despair. We must be intentional about always fixing our eyes on Jesus, especially in hard situations. How do we keep our eyes fixed on Jesus in hard times? By reading our Bibles, worshiping, and praying.

Do you find yourself focusing on the storm or your Savior? Do you frantically try to find a solution to the problem through research or other means? Or do you shut down and lose the ability to function at all when faced with adversity? Jesus is always with you and always the perfect place to focus your gaze. If you struggle with focusing on him in the storm, ask for his help.

> **PRAYER**: *Father God, thank you for providing peace and hope in hard times. Thank you for being a life-saving buoy to keep my eyes fixed on to stay on course in life. Please help me keep my eyes fixed on you, to stay in my Bible, to be fervent in prayer, and to always worship you. In Jesus' name, amen.*

Day 14

Trusting God Without Understanding

Trust in the Lord with all your heart and lean not on your own understanding. In all your ways, acknowledge him, and he will make your paths straight.
—PROVERBS 3:5-6

This is one of my all-time favorite verses. If we could live by this one principle—trusting God with all our heart and not leaning on our own understanding—our lives would be so much more peaceful. But doing this is often difficult when life's distractions and struggles get in the way.

Life's distractions include the responsibilities we juggle in our personal lives, careers, families, and ministries. They also include the constant pull of social media and news vying for our attention. Distractions come in the form of worries, disappointments, frustrations, and the physical pains we battle daily.

I don't know if you struggle with this next part like I do, but in addition to life's distractions, I wrestle with a strong desire to understand. I'm a big researcher. I LOVE learning and trying to understand everything I can about the Bible, God, life, humanity, theology, and this world.

Yet, we serve and love a God who, in many ways, is beyond understanding. This has been one of the most challenging aspects of my Christian walk—not understanding why God does what he does, or why he doesn't do the things I think he should do. Can you relate?

When we get caught in the whirlwind of trying to figure God out, we need to step back and remember this verse. Trusting God doesn't require understanding him. Instead of trying to comprehend his ways, we should recall the countless times he has been good to us.

Remember all the ways he has proven himself worthy of your trust. Then, ask him to help you trust him more and release your need to understand. These intentional prayers will always bring you peace and reassurance that God is good, and that everything will be okay—even when you don't understand.

> **PRAYER**: *Heavenly Father, thank you for being the most trustworthy person in my life. Thank you for never wavering or failing me. Please help me trust you more, and not struggle to try so hard to understand you. I place my life in your hands and trust you with it all completely. In Jesus' name, amen.*

Day 15

Unshakable!

*I keep my eyes always on the Lord. With
him at my right hand, I will not be shaken.
—PSALM 16:8*

A favorite summer activity with my kids is playing a game in the lake with my paddleboard. My two teenagers and I climb onto the board and do our best to shake and tip it, trying to make each other fall into the water. It's a blast, and they usually both fall off over and over again. I'm usually the one who stays firmly on the board because I keep my eyes focused on my kids, anticipating their movements.

That game is a fun kind of shaking, unlike the challenges in our lives that shake us and threaten to drown us in our circumstances. I've had plenty of times when I've faced trials or tough situations, and my eyes have too quickly shifted from the Lord to the problem in front of me. When that happens, it takes a toll on my mental, spiritual, and physical well-being. I'm sure you've experienced that too.

There's a reason the Bible reminds us so many times to always keep our eyes fixed on the Lord. That's how we stay focused on what is good and avoid being overwhelmed by our circumstances. It's how we remain strong when life weakens us. Keeping our eyes on the Lord—always—means staying connected to him through prayer, Bible reading, worship, and expressing gratitude.

What's the benefit of doing so? We are strengthened and made unshakable. Yes, please!

I admit there have been trials, like my son's cancer, that shook me at first—quite a bit, actually. I felt shaken because I took my eyes off God and focused on the situation. I fixated on all the things that could go wrong during brain surgery or chemotherapy, or the fear of the cancer returning. My mind spiraled into the "what ifs" instead of resting in the goodness and truth of God. That choice left me feeling shaken. But when God helped me realign my focus on him, I became strong and steady again, able to withstand the blows from life and the enemy.

So, I challenge you: if you've taken your eyes off God in the midst of your hard circumstances, refocus on him today. Ask him to help you, because sometimes it feels impossible to do on your own. He is ready and willing to help you fix your gaze back on him!

***PRAYER**: Heavenly Father, thank you for giving me a way to be unshakable in this crazy life. Thank you that I can focus my eyes and thoughts on you and you are always by my right hand. Please help me to keep my eyes ALWAYS focused on the you and not drift to my circumstances. In Jesus' name, amen.*

Day 16

Press Pause on Worry

So we don't look at the troubles we can see now; rather, we fix our gaze on things that cannot be seen. For the things we see now will soon be gone, but the things we cannot see will last forever.
—2 CORINTHIANS 4:18

Science teaches us that we can't focus on both gratitude and worry at the same time. This is a gift from God because it means we have the choice of where to direct our thoughts. If we choose to focus on gratitude, worry cannot take hold of our minds.

I'll admit, the last few days have been more challenging than usual for me to keep my eyes fixed on the Lord. I've had to be more intentional about speaking gratitude and praise. Yesterday marked my son's 18th chemotherapy infusion and the 43rd week of treatment for his second battle with cancer.

For a couple of days, I found myself reflecting on everything he and our family have endured. My thoughts kept returning to all the medical procedures, surgeries, infusions, hospital stays, insomnia, nerve pain, emotional trauma, and more. I was also fixating on the side effects of chemo that we'll need to address once his treatment ends. The journey is far from over for us.

Even though it's been harder to focus on God's goodness, it hasn't been impossible. Several times I've stopped the negative thoughts from filling my mind and have intentionally shifted my focus by speaking praises and recalling God's goodness. I've reminded myself of his promises in scripture and reflected on the great things the Lord has done.

There are plenty of troubles before me—not just my son's cancer journey—that I could fix my gaze on, as this verse warns against. But with the power of the Holy Spirit, I choose to set my focus on the spiritual things I cannot see with my physical eyes.

I'm sure you can relate: it's so easy to get caught up in the hard things you face daily in the physical realm. Shifting your focus to what you can't physically see—God's presence, truth, love, and goodness—can feel unnatural. But it's necessary. You can make this shift by regularly reading and recalling scripture, speaking aloud the things you are grateful for, keeping a gratitude journal, praying, soaking in worship music, and surrounding yourself with people who encourage you to focus on the good.

I encourage you to be intentional about your thoughts and where you fix your gaze. Pause the negative and worrisome thoughts, and press play on worship music, praise to God, prayer, and scripture. You'll be amazed at how much better you feel after a praise session compared to a worry session!

> **PRAYER**: *Dear Father, thank you for creating my mind so I can only focus on either worry or praise. Please help me be intentional about pausing the worry and playing the praise in my mind. In Jesus' name, amen.*

Day 17

Laser Focused

You will keep in perfect peace all who trust in you, all whose thoughts are fixed on you!
—ISAIAH 26:3 (NLT)

When I was a firearms instructor, I loved teaching people the fundamentals of shooting. One of the key fundamentals is called sight alignment, which involves where the shooter focuses their eyes—on the gun sights and the target. To shoot accurately, the person must stay focused on the sights and target while slowly squeezing the trigger to avoid jerking the gun and missing the shot.

Many people struggled with maintaining this laser focus. They were easily distracted by other elements of shooting or the activity around them at the range. I had them practice repeatedly to train their focus despite distractions. With enough practice, they became consistent and hit the target every time.

This kind of laser focus is also vital in our spiritual lives. It's what has helped our family not just survive but thrive during 2.5 years of navigating our childhood cancer journey. We've worked hard to stay laser-focused on God and his promises. But honestly, just like my shooting students, there are times when our focus falters, and we miss the target of God's peace, hope, and joy. Thankfully, more often than not, God graciously helps us refocus on him.

Another reason our family makes it through hard times is because we don't aim for the unrealistic target of expecting an easy life. Such expectations can be devastating when trials come, and they're not biblical. Instead, we aim to trust in God's promises and recognize the goodness that can emerge from trials like this cancer journey. So much goodness has come, even in the midst of pain.

In your own hard times, I pray that you keep your eyes, heart, and mind laser-focused on the target of God and his promises. He alone can provide you with peace, joy, and hope in the hardest of trials. I also pray that as you focus on God, you overflow with so much hope that people around you are drawn to ask how you can have hope even when life is hard.

> ***PRAYER***: *Dear Father, thank you for your peace and your plan. Thank you for always being there for me to fix my eyes upon and always responding with peace. Please help me to stay focused on you in the good and bad times. In Jesus' name, amen.*

Day 18

The Power of Praise

Praise the Lord, my soul: all my inmost being, praise His holy name. Praise the LORD, my soul, and forget not all His benefits — who forgives all your sins and heals all your diseases, who redeems your life from the pit and crowns you with love and compassion. —PSALM 103:1-4

One evening, a close friend and I were talking on the phone. I was curled up on the couch, and we were sharing the challenges we'd been facing. I have to admit, it wasn't a pretty conversation.

We were supporting each other and commiserating, but it wasn't uplifting or bringing glory to God. Honestly, we were being negative and complaining—yuck. That's hard to admit because I rarely speak like that. But at that moment, I was worn down, mentally, physically, and emotionally exhausted. I wanted my life to look different. I desired no more childhood cancer, teen depression, physical pain, or emotional heartache.

Midway through the conversation, I stopped us and acknowledged how negative we'd become. I said, *"Let's pause and praise God for whatever goodness comes to mind."* So, we did.

We praised him for our children and husbands. We praised him for our health and homes. We praised him for our friendship and church families. We even praised him for the very breath in our lungs.

For several minutes, we lifted up our praises, and you know what happened? The entire atmosphere shifted. I went from feeling heavy and despairing to feeling joy, gratitude, hope, and peace. There is power in praise!

I encourage you, no matter what you're facing, to stop the negative words before they come out of your mouth and replace them with praises to God for his goodness. Praise is a powerful way to fix your eyes on Jesus. Praise him for anything and everything you can think of—nothing is too small or simple to be thankful for.

> **PRAYER**: *Father God, thank you for the power of praise. Thank you that I can speak words of praise and you fill me with your hope, love, peace, and joy. Please help me speak more words of praise and fewer words of complaint or worry. In Jesus' name, amen.*

Day 19

Worship Over Worry

But seek first his kingdom and his righteousness, and all these things will be given to you as well. —MATTHEW 6:33

I love this verse—actually, the entire passage. Jesus is speaking to his disciples about worry, reassuring them that God will provide all they need. There's no reason to worry because God cares, is all-powerful, and is faithful.

Being the practical person I am, when I read this verse, I often think, "What do I tangibly need to do to seek God first?" Maybe you've asked the same question. So, let's look at the biblical foundation of what it means to seek God first.

I used to fail at seeking God first when bad news came my way. When my daughter was diagnosed with Tourette's Syndrome at five years old, my world felt like it was turned upside down. I was overwhelmed with tears, insomnia, and a loss of appetite. I spent weeks desperately researching every possible remedy.

I would pray occasionally, but I was operating from a place of desperation—apart from God—trying to control everything on my own. I wasn't seeking him first. Thankfully, Tourette's turned out not to be a huge deal, and today, she's doing great with no need for treatment.

Contrast my response back then with how I responded when my son was recently diagnosed with cancer for the second time. I cried, of course—there's no way to sugarcoat how devastating it is for your child to get cancer once, let alone twice. But this time, I had peace.

What caused this difference? A stronger reliance on God and a more intentional practice of keeping my eyes fixed on him through the storm. I seek God first now by surrendering my will to his, praying consistently, listening to worship music, speaking words of gratitude, reading daily devotions and the Bible, and connecting with close friends.

Now, before you think I'm unrelatable or super spiritual (please don't), let me assure you—I don't do all these practices perfectly every day. There were days when I was just trying to survive, crying through the unknowns while we had to decide whether to do chemotherapy or not. But most days, I've found a way to connect with the Lord, and I know this has made all the difference in how I responded to my son's cancer journey versus my daughter's Tourette's diagnosis.

When you consistently pray, read the Bible, fill your mind with worship music, surrender your will, and gather with godly friends, you are seeking first the Kingdom of God. And he will honor that effort in your life.

> **PRAYER**: *Father God, thank you for providing everything I need in life. You are such a good Father. Please help me keep my eyes fixed on you and to worship, not worry when faced with hard times. In Jesus' name, amen.*

Day 20

Hide and Seek

You will seek me and find me when you seek me with all your heart.
—JEREMIAH 29:13

A favorite family game of ours is hide and seek. We love to play indoors, outdoors, and even in the dark. Our house isn't huge, so finding a great hiding spot can be challenging—especially for my husband. At 6'3" with a sturdy build, there are very few places where he can completely hide.

Usually, a door is left ajar, a foot hangs out, a shoulder peeks from behind a wall, or a blanket is puffed up conspicuously. But he has shared with me that he enjoys being just a little visible because he ultimately wants our kids to find him. The game would become tiring and boring if they searched endlessly without success. But oh, the giggles and joy they exude are priceless as they search room to room and finally find Dad—because he isn't fully hidden.

I've always imagined that's how God is. He "hides" just enough for us to pursue him, but not so much that we can't find him. Our seeking reveals our heart's desire to find him and be with him. And when we seek him, he rewards us by allowing us to find him. He is such a good Father. I believe he wants us to seek him with joy in our hearts, not out of obligation.

But how do we seek him and find him? This is where the practical side of me kicks in again. We seek and find God by being intentional with our time, thoughts, and actions. We make it a priority to read his Word, fix our thoughts on him, talk to him throughout the day, and align our lives toward him.

Today's verse says, "*with all your heart.*" That's a tall order and one we can't accomplish on our own. As humans, we are constantly pulled in different directions and distracted by countless things. That's why we need the Holy Spirit's help. We must ask him daily—even regularly throughout the day—to help us seek the Lord with all our hearts.

"*All your heart*" means involving every aspect of your life: your family, dating, marriage, or singleness, parenting, careers, hobbies, and ministries—everything. Many things in life compete for your attention, but you can ask the Holy Spirit to keep you God-focused in the middle of it all. What area of your life do you need to ask the Holy Spirit to help you seek God more?

> **PRAYER**: *Heavenly Father, thank you for allowing me to find you and for being a Father who wants a relationship with me. Please help me seek after you with all my heart. In Jesus' name, amen.*

Reflection and Life Application

1) What verse from this section was most meaningful to me? *(Write it out here)* _____
_____
_____
_____
_____

2) What did I learn about fixing my eyes on Jesus that I didn't know before? Or what truth was I reminded of? _____
_____
_____
_____
_____

3) What from this section on focusing on Jesus encouraged me and brought me hope? _____
_____
_____
_____
_____

4) How has my perspective about focusing on Jesus in my storms changed since reading through this section? _____
_____
_____
_____
_____

5) What keeps me from fixing my eyes on Jesus and what steps will I take to change that? _____

_____
_____
_____
_____

6) Any other thoughts or takeaways about fixing my eyes on Jesus? _____

_____
_____
_____
_____
_____
_____
_____
_____

PRAYER: *Heavenly Father, thank you for your promises and truths about fixing my eyes on Jesus. Please help me take what you've shown me through this section on focusing my attention and apply it to my life. Help me keep my eyes fixed on Jesus and not my circumstances. In Jesus' name, amen.*

Section 4

Reflections and Daily Devotions for Grasping God's Sovereignty

GRASPING GOD'S SOVEREIGNTY

Our teenage son is fixated on understanding. He is brilliant, with a deep love for learning and a knack for visualizing how machines work and how life operates in general. Often, we ask him to do something without offering an explanation. As parents, we simply expect him to obey, even if he doesn't understand. However, his drive to understand often delays his obedience as he sits there questioning why we've asked him to do what we have.

As I write this, I realize where he gets it from—I'm the same way. I've always had a deep desire to understand, especially when it comes to why God does what he does. I've wrestled with him in hard seasons, trying to make sense of the pain and hurt. But God often remains silent, revealing his plan only later. Each trial I've faced has taught me more about his sovereignty.

Learning about and accepting God's sovereignty have been two of the most pivotal steps in growing my faith and trust in him. One of the hardest parts of suffering is not understanding why it's happening. The "why" questions seem endless, and the lack of answers can be heartbreaking.

I'm sure your mind has, at times, been filled with questions asking God, "Why?" When our thoughts spiral with impossible questions, we must fall back on what we do know: God is good, and ultimately, he is sovereign. He knows all, controls all, and has a plan and way of thinking far beyond ours.

If we could fully understand how God works, he wouldn't be God.

Acknowledging God's sovereignty has calmed my weary heart many times. Falling into his embrace, without more questions, just resting in his power, knowledge, and plan—without needing all the answers—has brought me peace and rest. I pray that you too can practice falling into his embrace, trusting in his sovereignty, and experiencing his peace in your storm.

God's sovereignty means he is the ultimate and final decision-maker over all creation. He is the Lord of lords and King of kings. No one and nothing has more power, authority, or control than him. While the enemy and humans are allowed some influence, God always has the final say. He is sovereign over all.

PRAYER: Heavenly Father, thank you for being all-knowing and in control of all. Thank you for continuing to guide and protect me even when I don't understand the hard parts of life. Please help me trust your sovereignty more and experience your peace through the storm. In Jesus' name, amen.

Day 21

A Comforting Promise

For just as the heavens are higher than the earth, so my ways are higher than your ways and my thoughts higher than your thoughts. —ISAIAH 55:9

As I write this devotion, I am sitting in Yosemite National Park, surrounded by towering cliffs. It's a majestic view that I'm blessed to experience every year. We camp at an elevation of around 4,000 feet, while the peaks rise even higher—over 8,000 feet.

Our family makes this trip annually, and our days are filled with swimming, hammock time, hiking, bike rides, card games, delicious food, and so much fun. Despite visiting every year, these towering peaks never fail to amaze me. Their massive heights fill me with awe.

This morning, as I walked and soaked in the glory of God's creation in these high peaks, I was reminded of today's verse. In the darkest moments of my suffering, when I've felt confused and desperate for understanding, this verse has been a lifeline for me time and time again.

Rarely have I gained an understanding of why I've suffered. But through this verse, God gently reminds me that his ways are far beyond my comprehension—and I need to be at peace with that. Often, I've spoken to myself or thought, *"God, I don't like what's happening and I don't understand, but I know your ways and thoughts are higher than mine."* These simple words bring me peace because he is sovereign, and I am not.

If you're feeling stuck, confused, or pleading with God for answers in the midst of a hard situation, I pray that you find comfort in this verse. He knows the suffering he has allowed in your life. He knows exactly what he is doing, the solution, and his plan for you. His ways and thoughts are higher than yours—and that's a good thing. Remember, if you could fully understand God, he wouldn't be God.

> **PRAYER**: *Father God, thank you that your thoughts and ways are higher than mine. Thank you that even if I don't understand you, I can trust you. Please help me accept that your ways are higher and to rest in that truth. In Jesus' name, amen.*

Day 22

Strength in Weakness

Three times I pleaded with the Lord to take it [the thorn] *away from me. But he said to me, "My grace is sufficient for you, for my power is made perfect in weakness." Therefore I will boast all the more gladly about my weaknesses, so that Christ's power may rest on me. That is why, for Christ's sake, I delight in weaknesses, in insults, in hardships, in persecutions, in difficulties. For when I am weak, then I am strong.* —2 CORINTHIANS 12:8-10

There remains a mystery in this passage about the "thorn" in Paul's life. Over the centuries, much speculation has arisen—was it a physical ailment, emotional turmoil, or persecution? Scripture doesn't give us a definitive answer. What we do know for certain is that Paul was deeply tormented by this thorn, so much so that he pleaded with the Lord three times to remove it.

Paul's pleading is incredibly comforting to me. Here was one of the greatest leaders in our Christian faith, suffering to the point of begging God to take away something that tormented him. That kind of desperation feels so relatable.

When our son faced multiple cancer diagnoses, brain surgery, and a year of chemotherapy, I pleaded with God over and over again. During my own battle with over thirty years of debilitating anxiety, I begged God to take it away. As I've dealt with a broken back, I have continually asked God to heal me. When our daughter was struggling with depression and anxiety, I cried out to God to remove those tormentors. As we experience the heartbreak and shock of rejection and a broken relationship, I plead with God to remedy it.

Yet, in each of these situations, God didn't respond with immediate healing, restoration, or relief. He made me wait—sometimes for a season, sometimes longer, sometimes still—to either remove the torment or reveal why he was allowing it to stay.

Over time, I've learned to find comfort in God's delay. Every time, I've discovered his strength in my weakness and his grace to be sufficient for me, just as it was for Paul. Do I like suffering? No. Would I choose it? Never. But God has an incredible way of using it to make me stronger and draw me closer to him.

You, too, like Paul, can find strength when you feel weak. You can experience peace even as you endure the thorn in your life. If God is choosing not to remove your thorn, trust that he has a reason. Rest, as Paul did, in God's sovereignty.

> ***PRAYER***: *Father, I admit I have thorns I want you to remove. I thank you for hearing my pleading for their removal. And I thank you for giving me strength when I am weak. Please help me see the purpose in my pain and your presence in my suffering. In Jesus' name, amen.*

Day 23

Become Like the Son

And we know that in all things God works for the good of those who love him, who have been called according to his purposes. For God knew his people in advance, and chose them to become like his son...
—ROMANS 8:28-29

I grew up playing competitive softball, training for several hours almost daily. Part of this training involved progressively harder drills to sharpen my skills. My coach would intentionally hit balls harder and farther to stretch my abilities and push me to the point of failure.

Failure was a regular part of my softball journey. Each time I failed, I learned what to adjust to grow as an athlete. My coach understood that the long, grueling drills—a "suffering" of sorts—were necessary to help me reach my goal of becoming a top player. In our spiritual journey, God is like our coach. his ultimate goal for us is to make us more like his Son, Jesus. Just as my coach knew the value of tough drills, God uses our struggles to refine us and help us grow.

Some of the greatest comforts we can find in God's sovereignty are knowing that he knows everything, he has a master plan, and that plan is good for his people. Our suffering is not random; but falls within his divine plan. Our trials aren't pointless tears, pain, heartache, or loss. They're not evidence of a God who is unaware of our lives or one who is being harsh. God uses these experiences to shape us into the likeness of Jesus, which should also be our ultimate goal.

Admittedly, if we were in charge, our plans for becoming more like Jesus would likely avoid pain and suffering altogether. But such a plan would be less effective and far from transformative. God knows better. He knows that hard trials refine us, deepen our prayer lives, increase our sensitivity to the Holy Spirit, and draw us closer to him—all of which guide us toward Christlikeness.

It's important to note something about Romans 8:28. Many people misunderstand this verse to mean that God will work all hard situations for their comfort as if the end result will always align with their idea of "good." But verse 29 clarifies God's purpose: his idea of "good" is to make us more like Jesus—not to make life comfortable or easy.

If you're like me, you naturally desire comfort and ease. But ultimately, you should embrace God's sovereignty and his plan to make you more like Jesus. And you must remember that part of this plan includes suffering with a purpose—just like the challenging drills in my softball training.

__PRAYER__: Father, thank you for your sovereignty. Thank you for wanting to make me more like Jesus. Please strengthen me to bear my suffering and represent your Son to the world. In Jesus' name, amen.

Day 25
On a Hospital Floor

Father, if you are willing, take this cup from me; yet not my will, but yours be done. —LUKE 22:42

It was 1:14 a.m., the day after our 10-year-old son's brain surgery to remove a tumor from his skull and the protective layer of his brain. He had already endured hours of complications from medications and had been rushed for a CT scan due to a possible brain bleed. Now, he faced yet another complication.

His system wasn't clearing the toxins from the anesthesia, and the nurses and doctors were unsure why. Nothing they tried was working. They informed us they would attempt one more technique, and if that didn't succeed, they would have to resort to a more drastic measure.

We had been praying fervently for days, believing and declaring that the surgery and recovery would go smoothly. We had declared, decreed, and commanded in Jesus' name what we expected to happen (a spiritual practice we no longer believe in). We had total faith that everything would go well. But it hadn't—and it wasn't.

At 1:30 a.m., desperate and weary, I got down on my knees in the hospital room and cried out to God, *"How am I supposed to pray?"* At that moment, a clear image of Jesus in the Garden of Gethsemane came to my mind. The words, *"Not my will but yours be done,"* were crystal clear in my thoughts.

I stood up, walked over to my son's bed, laid my hands on his abdomen, and prayed, *"God, please make his body work right, yet not my will but yours be done."* Just a few minutes later, our son woke up and said he had to pee—and miraculously, he did! I have prayed that way ever since.

Now, I don't want you to see this as a secret formula for getting what you want. Ultimately, it comes down to God choosing how he answers prayer, and sometimes he still doesn't answer the way we hope. He is God, and his plans are higher than ours.

"Your will be done" are four of the most powerful words we can pray. They are the very words Jesus used, and he is our ultimate role model. When I pray those words, I release all responsibility for the outcome into God's hands. I can't control much anyway, but he is in control of everything.

I challenge you, the next time you pray for God to act, to include the words "not my will but your will be done." You may be surprised by the peace that comes over you when you release control and expectations to him. And you may also be amazed by the outcomes that flow from those humble and mighty words.

> **PRAYER**: *Heavenly Father, thank you for your will. Thank you that it is good and that you are in control. Help me trust you with the outcomes of my suffering and always pray that YOUR will be done in my circumstances and life. In Jesus' name, amen.*

Day 26

In the Potter's Hands

Yet you, Lord, are our Father. We are the clay, you are the potter; we are all the work of your hand. —ISAIAH 6:8

I homeschool my kids, and one day we were making pottery using a pottery wheel. My son, who loves miniature things, created a tiny vase, pitcher, and bowl. His purpose for these items was to use them for mini-cooking, so he designed and shaped them in a way that best suited his plan.

As we worked, I thought about how strange it would be if the pitcher, as the created vessel, could speak up and say it should have been made differently or had a purpose other than holding water. The pitcher was designed and created by my son, the creator, for a specific purpose. It was carefully planned and made.

How often do we, the created, speak or act as though our Creator God made a mistake in our design or purpose? How often do we question a situation or suffering in our lives as if God allowed it by accident? Today's verse reminds us that everything in the universe, seen and unseen, was created by him and for him. Like my son's tiny water pitcher, we are vessels created for God's purposes.

This means that in his infinite wisdom and sovereignty, God perfectly designed us and planned our lives for his purposes. So, who are we to question the all-knowing Creator and his plans? Our successes and failures, joys and sufferings, careers, relationships, and families—all are part of his purpose.

You can rest in the truth that God created you just as you are, for his reasons. And ask him how you can best use what you have and where you are to fulfill his will. Afterall, you are clay in the Master's hands.

> **PRAYER**: *Father God, thank you for your sovereignty and your perfect plan for my creation and life. Thank you that I am not just a random blip on the earth that you don't care about. Please help me be grateful for who I am and where you have placed me as one of your intentionally created vessels. In Jesus' name, amen.*

Day 27

Not Because of My Sin

"It was not because of his sins or his parents' sins," Jesus answered. "This happened so the power of God could be seen in him." —JOHN 9:3

When our son was first diagnosed with cancer, some of the people who prayed with us said something that wasn't very supportive. They asked us to search our hearts for and pray against any personal sin that might have caused this terrible thing to happen to our child.

My husband and I understand that sin has consequences, and we humbly admit that we are neither perfect nor sinless. However, we do not believe that our sin caused our son to get cancer. Still, we were desperate to do everything we could to help him, so, just in case, we repented of all our past and present sins. Yet, he still wasn't healed.

Our belief is rooted in what the Bible teaches: we live in a fallen and broken world, and cancer is a part of that fallenness. God allows suffering, like cancer and other struggles, for many reasons. Scripture is full of examples where people endured suffering for God's glory and purposes.

This verse from John brought my husband and me immense peace after those conversations. We were reassured that our son's cancer was not a result of our sin, just as the man's blindness in the passage was not due to his or his parent's sin. God had already given us clarity on this, and he confirmed it again when someone else prayed with us and quoted this very verse. God allowed our son's cancer so he could bring glory through our story.

And indeed, God has been glorified through our son's two-and-a-half-year battle with cancer. He has changed false beliefs, drawn us closer to himself, strengthened our family's faith, and given us the opportunity to help others who are suffering. Through our story, people have come to salvation, our prayer lives have been transformed, our reliance on God has grown, and his ultimate sovereignty has been emphasized.

This verse also highlights God's sovereignty by showing that he allowed the man's blindness so his glory could be displayed through the man's healing.

If you know your suffering is the result of your own sin or choices, then repent and allow God to cleanse your heart and life. But if you, like us, are certain that your suffering is not a consequence of sin but rather something God has allowed for his glory and purposes, rest in his sovereignty and plan. Allow him to use your suffering in every possible way to bring good to you and to others.

PRAYER*: Father God, I thank you again for your sovereignty. Thank you for having a purpose and plan for the hard things you allow. Thank you for refining and shaping me through them. Please help me go through suffering in a way that makes your glory shine. In Jesus' name, amen.*

Reflection and Life Application

1) What verse from this section was most meaningful to me? *(Write it out here)* _____
_____
_____
_____
_____

2) What did I learn about God's sovereignty that I didn't know before? Or what was I reminded of that I already knew? _____
_____
_____
_____
_____

3) What from this section on God's sovereignty encouraged me and brought me hope? _____
_____
_____
_____
_____

4) How has my perspective on God's sovereignty changed since reading through this section? _____
_____
_____
_____
_____

5) Is it hard for me to fully surrender control to God and trust his sovereignty? Why or why not? _____

_____
_____
_____
_____

6) Any other thoughts or takeaways about God's sovereignty? _____

_____
_____
_____
_____
_____
_____
_____

***PRAYER**: Heavenly Father, thank you for your promises and truths about your sovereignty. Please help me to take what you've shown me through this section on your sovereignty and apply it to my life. Help me to fully trust you and truly believe that you are in control of my life and have good plans for me, whether life looks good at the time or not. In Jesus' name, amen.*

Section 5

Reflections and Daily Devotions for Having Faith Over Fear

FAITH OVER FEAR

Illogical fear used to debilitate me—literally freezing me in place. It limited my social life, spiritual gifts, and overall joy. Ever since I was a child, I was bound by illogical fear and anxiety. Fear of being kidnapped or attacked. Fear of someone breaking into my house. Fear of my children being killed or getting an incurable disease. The fears seemed endless.

My thoughts would spiral into a cycle of "what ifs." What if my husband gets killed at work? What if my kids play outside and someone takes them? What if my husband loses his job? What if people don't like what I say? The spiral was exhausting and immobilizing.

I know I'm not the only one who has battled the debilitating effects of illogical fear. I specify "illogical" because not all fear is bad. God gave us a fear response to keep us safe from actual threats, like vicious animals chasing us in the wild or a car that almost hits us in the street. But too often, people get trapped in their thoughts of bad things that could happen but rarely ever do. Those thoughts torment them and steal their joy, purpose, relationships, health, and more.

Today, I can say that I "used to" be bound by fear because God has fully set me free from that imprisonment. I now have faith over fear, even in the hardest of times. And I pray that you experience that freedom as well.

My most massive breakthrough, which brought total freedom from fear and anxiety, was through deliverance and inner healing ministry. This is a topic for another book but there is a real segment of the spiritual realm—Satan and his demons—whose goal is to steal, kill, and destroy everything good in your life. They want to bring destruction to your peace, sanity, career, relationships, health, joy, finances, and hope.

When the influence of those evil spiritual powers was broken over my life and the truth and victory of Jesus were declared, I was no longer a victim to fear and anxiety.

Since being set free from the torment of illogical fear, I've found the practice of meditating on and reciting scripture to be a powerful weapon. When I recognize fearful or anxious thoughts trying to creep into my mind, I speak aloud many of the verses in this section.

Although God has set me free from illogical fear, the battle with fear remains one of the most common struggles that I help fellow Christians overcome. If you struggle with a stronghold of fear, I hope this section will be helpful for you too.

PRAYER: *Father God, thank you for your constant reassurance to not be afraid. Thank you for being trustworthy, mighty, and able to do the impossible. Help me to be free from the grips of fear. In Jesus' mighty name, amen.*

Day 28

Free From Fear

*I prayed to the Lord, and he answered me.
He freed me from all my fears.
—PSALM 34:4*

I used to be a firearms instructor, and it was one of the most incredible and fun jobs I've ever had. I trained many people who battled significant fears—fear of guns, fear of being attacked, fear of active shooters in public places, home invasions, kidnappings, rape, and more. I understood their struggles because I, too, battled many of those fears for over thirty years.

Even as a firearms instructor and personal safety trainer, I suffered from debilitating fear. While I had the confidence to stop a threat if necessary, fear oppressed me in my home and personal life every single day. At times, it was absolutely suffocating.

No amount of personal defense or firearms training could get rid of that fear. No self-help book, willpower, or hours of counseling ever helped me overcome it. It wasn't until I prayed to God to take it away and stopped willful sin in my life that I was finally broken free from the bondage of fear.

Today, I can honestly say I no longer struggle with fear at all. Even in deeply fear-inducing situations—like when my child had cancer and needed brain surgery—I have experienced complete peace. By the grace, goodness, and power of God, I no longer live in fear or am hindered by it in any way.

One clarification I always made in my firearms classes is that God gave us the gift of fear as a tool to save our lives in life-threatening situations. Healthy fear is what makes us aware of dangers, like looking both ways before crossing the street or reacting appropriately when facing a real threat, such as encountering a bear in the woods. This kind of fear triggers the fight-or-flight response and keeps us alive.

However, too often, people become bound by illogical fears—fears that are irrational and usually never come to pass. These are the types of fears that hinder our lives, and they are the ones God frees us from.

Do you struggle with illogical fears? Do you get caught in the "what if" spiral of negative and irrational thinking? I hear you. I've been there. But I want to speak hope into your life that you can be set free from that stronghold forever. Begin by crying out to God for freedom from fear. And declare today's verse as truth in your life.

> ***PRAYER***: *Dear God, thank you that you have the power and desire to set me free from my fears. Please help break the bondage of fear over my mind and life so that I can walk in true freedom. In Jesus' name, amen.*

Day 29

How to Stop Your Racing Thoughts

We demolish arguments and every pretension that sets itself up against the knowledge of God, and we take captive every thought and make it obedient to Christ. —2 CORINTHIANS 10:5

We recently got a one-year-old German Shepherd puppy. She is a power-packed ball of energy that can be uncontrollable. She also doesn't know many basic commands yet. So, when I want to get control of her to take her for a walk or train her, I have to first capture her as she frantically runs around.

Sometimes, when she is running around crazy, she damages things. Once our puppy is captured, I can hold her in my arms and better control her to do whatever I need her to do.

Your thoughts are similar to our puppy. They can be wild and racing through your mind, uncontrolled. If left unchecked, they can cause damage to yourself, others, your faith, and your life. Often, I assume, your thoughts are filled with fear and anxiety, just like mine used to be.

I've already mentioned my struggle for over thirty years with debilitating fearful and anxious thoughts. Thoughts about terrible things happening would cripple my actions and demolish my peace and joy. I operated most of the time out of a state of fear and was controlled by those anxious thoughts.

Even as a Christian, deep in prayer and Bible reading, I still couldn't stop the racing, fearful thoughts. That is until I learned 2 Corinthians 10:5 and how to take my thoughts captive—and how we have power over the enemy and his tactics in our minds.

I created what I call the "3-Second Rule" to take my thoughts captive and make them obedient to Christ. We can't control what thoughts enter our minds, but we can stop them from racing and ruminating. We do this by holding them captive and seeing if they line up with the Word of God. When a thought enters my mind, I take it captive, just like a prisoner being taken to jail. Did I come up with this thought? Is this something God would be saying to me? Does this thought line up with the Bible? Is it loving and guiding, or rude and condemning?

This practice of capturing and questioning my thoughts takes only a few seconds. I then decide either to reject the thought because it is from the enemy and will be harmful, or to accept it and allow it to enter my mind for good.

Tomorrow, I will share the main scripture I run my thoughts by and give you some examples of how to use this invaluable tool in your life. Because you don't have to fall victim to uncontrolled, terrible thoughts. The more you practice this simple method of capturing your thoughts, the easier it will become.

> ***PRAYER***: *Father God, thank you for the divine weapons to fight the tactics of the enemy. Please help me stop the racing thoughts in my head and focus more on you. In Jesus' name, amen.*

Day 30

A Simple Mental Checklist

And now, dear brothers and sisters, one final thing. Fix your thoughts on what is true, and honorable, and right, and pure, and lovely, and admirable. Think of things that are excellent and worthy of praise. —PHILIPPIANS 4:8

I love a good checklist. Give me a list, and I feel like my mind is clearer. Even with all our modern technology, I still make my grocery list on paper.

Yesterday, I shared about taking our thoughts captive. Today, I'll share a simple checklist to help make our thoughts obedient to Christ. Remember, we have just three seconds to take a thought captive and either accept or reject it. A simple way to determine whether we should accept or reject a thought is to run it by the checklist in today's verse.

For a practical example, I'll share when I used to struggle with debilitating fear. For instance, I would imagine my little kids being kidnapped, drugged, raped, and killed. I battled these thoughts ALL THE TIME.

Here's how to take the thought captive and run it through our biblical checklist. When a bad thought enters my mind, I take it captive—locking it in a jail cell—rather than allowing my mind to run wild. Then I ask myself: "*Is this thought true, honorable, right, pure, lovely, admirable, excellent, and worthy of praise?"* Um, no. Once I recognize that it's a bad thought, I reject it.

Usually, with that simple effort, the thought goes away, and I can move on. But sometimes, if the thought is very intrusive, or if I'm overwhelmed or tired, I'll have to repeat the process and pray for the Lord to take the thought away. Over the years, I've found that the more I practice this, the easier it gets.

Fear may not be the biggest challenge you face with your thoughts. Perhaps you struggle more with thoughts of lust, addiction, anger, doubt, shame, jealousy, or insecurity. Whatever thoughts you wrestle with, you can become a slave to your negative thoughts, which ultimately leads to becoming a slave to fear, rejection, lust, addiction, jealousy, or other struggles.

I want to challenge you to practice the "3-Second Rule." You don't have to be a slave to negative thinking. God has given you the ability to control your thoughts and decide which ones to dwell on. I recommend memorizing this verse and printing it out to hang around your living spaces so you can easily reference it when needed.

> ***PRAYER***: *Father God, thank you for being the authority in my life to help control my thoughts. Thank you for the simple checklist in your Bible to help me align my thoughts with your word. Please help me when I feel weak or overwhelmed to take my thoughts captive and make them obedient to you. In Jesus' name, amen.*

Day 31

Fear Not, The Battle Belongs to the Lord

₁₅ He said, "Listen, ...This is what the Lord says: Do not be afraid! Don't be discouraged by this mighty army, for the battle is not yours but God's.... ₁₇ You will not have to fight this battle. Take up your positions; stand firm and see the deliverance the Lord will give you, Judah and Jerusalem. Do not be afraid; do not be discouraged. Go out to face them tomorrow, and the Lord will be with you...."
—2 CHRONICLES 20:15, 17

We were three months into the first battle with our son's cancer. One brain surgery, four tough days in the hospital, another surgery, too many medical tests to count, and now scans to see if the cancer had spread. It felt like a battle and a huge opportunity for fear to take over. While we waited in the hospital for scans, a friend texted me, "I think this is for you. 2 Chronicles 20:17."

I looked up the verse, and it was a clear message from the Lord: "You will not have to fight this battle. Take up your positions; stand firm and see the deliverance the Lord will give you..." Right there in the hospital room, I said aloud, "AMEN! Our battle belongs to the Lord. I don't need to be afraid. God will fight for us and our son."

Then I continued reading a book I'd brought to the hospital. Ten minutes into my reading, right there on the page was 2 Chronicles 20:15! I thought, *"Lord, are you trying to send me a message?!"* We sure felt like we were facing a vast army of unknowns. I opened up 2 Chronicles and read all of chapter 20. I suggest you do the same. It is powerful!

The story is about King Jehoshaphat, who was about to be attacked by three enemy armies. He fell on his knees before God, fearful, and asked for help. A man told the King not to be afraid, that it was God's battle, not his. So, the King organized his people to praise God instead of fight.

The story ends a few verses later, saying every enemy was killed. God brought them victory without them fighting at all! The King did not try to fight his own battle, nor did he freeze in fear.

What battles are you facing right now that you need to let God fight instead of trying to control them? Prayer and praise are powerful weapons for our battles, and they conquer fear. These two weapons place the battle in God's hands. He is the only one capable of victory, has all knowledge of what's going on in your battle, and is all-powerful.

> **PRAYER**: *Heavenly Father, thank you for fighting my battles. Thank you for this story of victory through prayer and praise. Please help me, in my impossible situations and times of fear, to fall on my knees before you with prayer and praise, and let you fight my battles. In Jesus' name, amen.*

Day 32

Standing on Solid Ground

I waited patiently for the Lord to help me, and he turned to me and heard my cry. He lifted me out of the pit of despair, out of the mud and the mire. He set my feet on solid ground and steadied me as I walked along. He has given me a new song to sing, a hymn of praise to our God. Many will see what he has done and be amazed. They will put their trust in the Lord. —PSALM 40:1-3

A few years ago, my kids participated in a mud run. They ran three miles and completed over 20 obstacles along the course. One of the most challenging was a long mud pit. The pit had low-hanging ropes and nets, forcing the kids to fully immerse themselves in the mud.

They struggled because the mud was almost sucking them deeper. They clawed and crawled, slowly but steadily. When they finally got to the end of the pit, they reached up and grabbed the hand of a man whose job was to pull them out of the mud. With one strong lift, he pulled them from the miry pit, and they stood on solid ground.

That mud run was a fun event for everyone involved. But the miry pit of depression and anxiety that my teen daughter was stuck in this year due to her brother's cancer was anything but fun. At times, it felt like pure terror and darkness. For those of you who have battled depression or anxiety, you know exactly what I'm talking about.

But just as she had a man pull her from the physical mud pit during the fun run, she had the Man named Jesus pull her out of the pit of depression and anxiety. He has worked miracles in her life and set her free from those battles. Now, she radiates the light, love, and joy of Jesus.

There is a new song in her mouth. I've already witnessed people trust the Lord because of her story. I believe today's passage perfectly describes her experience: she was overcome by anxiety and depression, but the Lord lifted her and gave her a new song.

He can do that for you too! He can lift you from the miry pit of fear, depression, anxiety, pain, insecurity, addiction, and more. He can set your feet on solid ground and give you a new song. Cry out to him—he will hear you and rescue you!

> ***PRAYER****: Father God, thank you for hearing my cries. Please lift me out of this miry pit and set my feet on solid ground. Please give me a new song so that people will praise you and be amazed. In Jesus' name, amen.*

Day 33

Be Strong and Courageous

So be strong and courageous! Do not be afraid and do not panic before them. For the Lord your God will personally go ahead of you. He will neither fail you nor abandon you. —DEUTERONOMY 31:6

Several years ago, when my daughter was six years old, we noticed her make some unusual movements and sounds. After many doctor visits and neurological tests, she was diagnosed with Tourette's Syndrome. This diagnosis turned my world upside down. What was wrong with my girl? What would this mean for her and our family? What was the treatment? At the time, I was still struggling with debilitating fear, and I was consumed by worry about this diagnosis.

A few days later, I attended a Christian women's conference and was a tearful wreck. Every speaker addressed trusting God in uncertainty and not giving in to fear. I almost got up and left because it hit me so deeply.

At the end of the conference, we were invited to go up front and choose a river rock from the stage. We were also told to pick up a piece of paper with a scripture on it and write that verse on the rock with a permanent marker. The instructions were to keep the rock in a place where we would regularly see it.

The verse on my paper was today's verse. It felt as if God was speaking directly to me through that piece of paper. I wrote the verse on the rock, and it still sits on my windowsill above my kitchen sink, a daily reminder not to be afraid because God is with me and in control.

Thankfully, my daughter's diagnosis ended up not being anything serious, and today we rarely notice it. And even more thankfully, God has set me free from that debilitating fear and anxiety. But the rock with the verse has helped me through many challenging and fearful moments since that conference and our girl's diagnosis.

Anytime you feel a fearful thought creeping in, you can recall this verse, and it will remind you that you have no reason to fear. God has gone ahead of you, and he won't fail you or leave you alone in your suffering. Oh, what a good God we have! You could even get your own rock and write the verse on it like I have. Then place it in a location you see regularly as your own reminder of God's goodness.

> ***PRAYER**: Father God, thank you for always being with me and going ahead of me in my trials. Please help me feel strong and courageous when I face hard times. In Jesus' name, amen.*

Reflection and Life Application

1) What verse from this section was most meaningful to me? *(Write it out here)* _____
_____
_____
_____
_____

2) What did I learn about having faith over fear that I didn't know before? Or what was I reminded of that I already knew? _____
_____
_____
_____
_____

3) What from this section on having faith over fear encouraged me and brought me hope? _____
_____
_____
_____
_____

4) How has my perspective on faith over fear changed since reading through this section? _____
_____
_____
_____
_____

5) What do I fear the most that I need to give over to God? _____
_____
_____
_____
_____

6) Any other thoughts or takeaways about faith over fear? _____
_____
_____
_____
_____
_____
_____
_____

PRAYER: *Heavenly Father, thank you for your promises and truths about having faith over fear. Please help me take what you've shown me through this section on having faith over fear and apply it to my life. Help my faith be bigger than my fears and help me keep declaring the truth that you are bigger than my fears. In Jesus' name, amen.*

Section 6

Reflections and Daily Devotions for Having Hope When Life's Hard

HOPE WHEN LIFE'S HARD

Hope is different for Christians than it is for non-believers. Non-believers often use the word "hope" when they really mean more of a wish. For example, "I hope this burger tastes good." "I hope he likes me." "I hope the jacket I want is on sale." "I hope I don't get sick." The list could go on. Non-believers put their hope in things like science, medicine, education, politicians, their own strength, the media, and many other sources.

The tragedy of putting hope in these things is that they all waver and fail us. Placing our hope in anything or anyone other than God and his promises will always leave us feeling hopeless in the end. As Christians, we must be intentional about not placing our hope in anything other than God and his promises.

We have an eternal hope that never wavers or lets us down. Hoping in God's promises is what keeps us going when we want to give up. Hope is knowing that, because of the Lord's promises, one day life will no longer be this hard.

Sometimes, life can feel so difficult that hope seems distant. I've heard many Christians say they are "hopeless," but that's impossible! A Christian can never be truly hopeless. They may feel hopeless, but that's because they have somehow disconnected from Hope himself, who lives inside them.

The verses in this section speak of having hope during our hard times because of God's promises. But our greatest hope is the eternal life that awaits us after this one—spending eternity with Jesus, where there will be no sorrow, suffering, pain, sadness, or tears. That is the eternal hope I cling to, and it keeps me hopeful even when life is hard.

Have you ever said the words, "I'm hopeless." Or, "This situation is hopeless." Maybe you have felt hopeless when life seems terribly hard. If so, I pray that this section reconnects you to the Hope that lives inside you, the Spirit of God. And I pray that you fully grasp the truth that you can never be hopeless as a child of God.

> ***PRAYER****: Heavenly Father, thank you for the gift of hope. Thank you that Hope himself lives inside me and I can never be hopeless. Please help me stay connected to the true source of Hope so I never feel hopeless again, even if my situation looks terrible. In Jesus' name, amen.*

Day 34

Rooted Deeply in Living Water

But blessed are those who trust in the Lord and have made the Lord their hope and confidence. They are like trees planted along a riverbank, with roots that reach deep into the water. Such trees are not bothered by the heat or worried by long months of drought. Their leaves stay green, and never stop producing fruit.
—JEREMIAH 17:7-8

I wish you could see the spectacular view in front of me as I write this devotion. I'm sitting comfortably on the riverbank of a beautiful, crystal-clear river in Yosemite National Park. The sun is peeking through the towering conifers and oaks that line the water's edge.

The trees are tall, lush, green, and full of life and strength. As I look at the waterline, I see hundreds of roots from the many trees reaching deeply into the fresh waters. I've been coming to this area for 35 years, and the trees always stand strong and healthy, deeply rooted in the river.

What you can be thankful you're not experiencing with me today is the high temperature of 102 degrees! Thankfully, just like the tree roots, my family stayed immersed in the cool waters of the river. Even with the high temperatures and occasional droughts, the trees along the river remain healthy and fruitful.

This scene is a great reminder of the promise in today's verse. When we stay spiritually rooted in the Living Water of Jesus, we will remain strong, healthy, and fruitful, even in the hard times of life. When the heat and droughts of life try to drain us and dry up our fruit, we can stay rooted in Jesus and remain strong and fruitful. The way we stay rooted in him is through prayer, worship, Bible reading, praise, and Christian community.

If you're feeling dried out, unfruitful, or unable to bear fruit, take a moment to check your spiritual practices. Are you doing the simple things—praying, worshiping, reading Scripture—that keep you connected to the Living Water of Jesus? If not, choose one and start today.

> **PRAYER**: *Thank you, Jesus, for being my Living Water; for giving me life and strength, and for helping me bear fruit even in the heat and droughts of life. Please help me stay rooted in you. In your mighty name, amen.*

Day 35

Hope From Suffering

Let us also glory in our sufferings, because we know that suffering produces perseverance; perseverance, character; and character, hope. —ROMANS 5:3-4

I am a big deal-finder when it comes to shopping. I don't like shopping just to shop, and I do everything I can to stay away from malls. But when we need something, I love finding a great deal. Whether it's 50% or more off an item or a buy-one-get-one-free deal, I'm elated to save us some money. It's even better when the seller throws in a gift or two with my purchase. I buy one item and walk away with four.

A bundle deal is what comes to mind when I read these verses. We often have to go through some sort of suffering (which costs us something in a way), but as a bundle deal, we come out of the experience with perseverance, character, and hope. In these short verses, we see multiple benefits to suffering!

Only God can do something like that. Only God can take something so hard and turn it into three wonderful gifts: perseverance, character, and hope.

I know we would all prefer our lives to be easy and comfortable, but do you seriously think we would ever grow our perseverance, character, and hope that way? Nope. It doesn't happen. We don't grow as much through ease and comfort as we do through trials and suffering. That's just the proven truth.

So, if you are in the middle of suffering, or the next time you are, ask God to help you choose the perspective that this verse promises. You will have greater perseverance, character, and hope. I'm praising God for that!

***PRAYER**: Lord, thank you for your "bundle-deal" plan for suffering. Suffering is hard, but I'm thankful for the benefits of greater perseverance, character, and hope. Thank you for always looking out for me. Please help me to keep this promise in mind during hard times. In Jesus' name, amen.*

Day 36

The Promise of a New Body

And we believers also groan, even though we have the Holy Spirit within us as a foretaste of future glory, for we long for our bodies to be released from sin and suffering. We too, wait with eager hope for the day when God will give us our full rights as his adopted children, including the new bodies he has promised us.
—ROMANS 8:23

Oh, the promise of a new body! How I long for that day. I sit here today with chronic and severe pain from a broken back, slipped vertebrae, pinched nerves, and almost no disc. On top of that, I have new chronic pain and loss of mobility from bulging discs and slipped vertebrae in my neck. This is not the super athletic, able body I've always been used to.

Every morning lately, I wake up with severe, limiting pain in my right foot, lower back, and neck. It takes a while to get moving in the mornings, with certain exercises and stretches to loosen up my body. I'm only 43 at the time of writing, and that feels abnormal for someone my age—especially someone who has been an avid, competitive endurance athlete most of their life.

Several mornings, I've found myself in tears before the Lord, asking for healing. And if healing doesn't come right now, I ask for perseverance and strength to face the daily pain and limited mobility.

Thankfully, my situation isn't as bad as some others, and I always find things to be thankful for that I CAN do. But the promise in this verse of a new body is wonderful!

I cling to the promise that one day I will have a body that doesn't hurt anymore, and I will be able to do all the activities I please. I long for the day when I will be released from suffering, as this verse says. I look forward with anticipation to that day, for everyone who is suffering from pain in their body or other ailments.

Even in the midst of chronic pain and in this body that's not working properly, God is good. He is faithful and worthy of my trust. I will continue to pray for healing and a return to the activities I love, but I will also continue to find things I can be thankful for and not focus on what I cannot do.

If you struggle with chronic physical pain or limited mobility, I encourage you to focus on what you can do. Stop dwelling on what you used to do but can't anymore. That negativity only builds up in your body and makes the situation worse. But when you find something to be thankful for and focus on that, it will help you feel more complete and accomplished.

> **PRAYER**: *Lord, I thank you for the promise of a new body in eternity with you. Thank you for the hope that promise brings me, that I won't always be suffering from chronic pain. Please help me find some things I can do and bring me joy through those. In Jesus' name, amen.*

Day 37

Overflowing with Hope

May the God of hope fill you with all joy and peace as you trust in him, so that you may overflow with hope by the power of the Holy Spirit. —ROMANS 15:13

We have an above-ground swimming pool that we fill and keep topped off with a garden hose. One day, I noticed how low the water level was, so I turned on the hose. I usually set an alarm on my phone to remind me to turn the water off, but before I could set the alarm, I got distracted, and the alarm never got set. I forgot about the running water. The next day, I discovered the pool was overflowing—oh no! The water had been running all night!

I ran down to turn it off and noticed how much water had flowed down the hillside, into the garden, blackberry bushes, pool equipment, walkways, and beyond. Nothing around the pool was left untouched by the overflowing water. Thankfully, nothing was damaged, and the plants actually flourished with the extra water in summer time.

Our lives are to be like that above-ground pool. God is like the garden hose, filling us with hope, joy, and peace so that we can overflow those blessings into the lives of others. He just keeps pumping it in, and we get to pour it out to bless those around us.

Throughout our childhood cancer journey, we have experienced this more times than we could have imagined. God continues to fill us with hope, peace, and joy, and we share that story of hope with others. Because of sharing our story, we've received hundreds of messages, comments, and calls from people who have been filled with hope, inspired, and seen their faith grow because of what we've shared.

Our journey has been hard—childhood cancer and chemo, brain surgery, teen anxiety and depression, chronic pain from a broken back, and more. But through it all, God has been so good, and we continue to share his goodness with others.

This overflow of hope starts with trusting God and doesn't come from your efforts; it comes from the Holy Spirit. You simply need to be a willing vessel, allowing God to keep filling you with hope so that you can overflow that abundance into the lives of others.

But God is a gentleman and he will not fill you if you are not willing or wanting him to. You must be intentional in coming to God to receive his filling. The more you come to him through prayer, worship, and Bible reading, the more he will pour into you. And then the more you will be able to pour into and bless others, just like my overflowing pool blessed the plants surrounding it.

***PRAYER**: Lord, thank you for your abundant gifts of hope, joy, and peace. Thank you that as your children, we can experience these gifts even in hard times. Please continue pouring them into me so I can overflow your goodness into other's lives. In Jesus' name, amen.*

Day 38

Resting on True Hope

*Let all that I am wait quietly before God,
for my hope is in him. He alone is my rock
and my salvation, my fortress where I will
not be shaken.* —PSALM 62:5-6

Due to our son's cancer, we've spent a couple of weeks in the hospital. This verse reminds me of those hospital stays, which remain some of the most intense emotional battles of his cancer journey.

For his jaw tumor, I recall facing a deep moment of hopelessness. The circumstances felt hopeless, but thankfully we were not hopeless because we had the unshakable hope of the Lord. The situation seemed bleak because the doctors decided that surgery was too risky and had no immediate plan. We had been counting on surgery to remove the rapidly growing tumor.

It was late at night, the primary medical team had gone home, and it was a three-day holiday weekend. We were left with a new resident who was unfamiliar with Jordan's case and lacked confidence in her role. She told us they would just do an hourly CT scan for a few days to track the tumor. That amount of radiation exposure would be extreme, and simply tracking the tumor as it ate through his bone was not a good option either.

I can't fully express the confusion, despair, and hopelessness in that hospital room. It was overwhelming. We weren't getting answers, and there was no plan to stop or remove the tumor. Those were some rough hours, waiting for a reply from the on-call doctor. I was frustrated at the lack of answers, but I was also filled with the hope of God.

I knew that even if the medical staff had no clarity, our God knew everything and would guide us in the right direction. In that moment, being so filled with hope in a hopeless situation, I felt an immense heaviness for those in the world who do not have the hope and peace of God in their lives. I felt a strong yearning to share the hope of Jesus with them. The truth is, no matter what they face, they can always have hope and peace through him.

So, I want to remind you of that truth as well. The "hope" that the medical field gives us is shakable. The "hope" from science, education, the media, and "experts" is also unstable. But the hope that God gives us is a solid rock that cannot be shaken. You can always count on God and rest in him to be your true source of hope and peace in hard times.

> ***PRAYER***: *Heavenly Father, thank you so much for being my true and solid source of hope, peace, and joy. Thank you for never failing me and always offering these gifts to me. Please help me seek after your true hope and not the false hope the world gives. In Jesus' name, amen.*

Day 39

Plans of Hope and a Future

"For I know the plans I have for you" declares the Lord "plans for your well-being, not for disaster, to give you a future and a hope." —JEREMIAH 29:11 (CSB)

Jeremiah was writing to the Jews who were living in captivity in a foreign country. They were far from home, struggling with the new normal, and had just been told a false prophecy that they would be able to return in two years. God dealt with the false prophet and spoke through Jeremiah, telling them they would be in exile for at least 70 years, so they better get settled in. The Jews were facing very hard times, physically and emotionally. They most likely wanted a quick fix and a return to normalcy. But that was not God's plan.

How often do you find yourself in hard situations that require establishing a new normal? How often are you facing trials and wishing for a quick fix? And how often does God reveal that a quick fix is not his plan, but that sitting with you through the hardship is? He shows you that he uses suffering and trials to refine and transform you, and to bring about better things for you and his Kingdom.

Although Jeremiah was addressing a situation that happened more than 500 years before Christ was born, these same promises of God apply to us today. God knows the plans he has for you. They are plans for your well-being and not for harm. They are plans to give you hope and a future.

These promises have carried me through some very difficult times in my life. Knowing that the Creator and Sustainer of the universe, my Lord and Savior, has good plans for me brings me a great deal of hope and peace. I can trust that even if I don't understand what's going on or why a particular trial is happening, God knows, and he has a purpose for it.

I also want to clarify that some translations use the word "prosper" in this verse. Prosper is often misunderstood and misused, especially when preached as financial prosperity. The Hebrew word translated as "prosper" here is *shalom* (pronounced "sha-LOM"), which has a much deeper and broader meaning. It signifies peace, completeness, welfare, safety, making things right, restoration, and fullness of life. These meanings are far superior for you than just financial gain!

> **PRAYER**: *Father God, thank you for having good plans for me and all your kids. Thank you for sitting with me in my hard seasons and using them for good. Help me focus on promises like those from today's verse instead of dwelling on the hard in hard times. In Jesus' name, amen.*

Day 40

Heard and Rescued

The righteous cry out, and the Lord hears them; he delivers them from all their troubles. The Lord is close to the brokenhearted and saves those who are crushed in spirit. The righteous person faces many troubles, but the Lord comes to the rescue each time. —PSALM 34:17-19

One sunny afternoon, I was outside in our yard when I heard one of my kids calling, "Mommy! Mommy! Help me!" I quickly walked toward the voice and found our young daughter stuck in a tree. Well, she wasn't physically stuck, but she was afraid to try to come down. Her fear had her frozen, feeling stuck.

I went over to her, offered words of encouragement, stretched my arms toward her, and lowered her safely from the tree. I held her tightly until she felt secure, and then, with a smile, she ran off to play.

I've recalled this scene many times in my own life, especially when facing traumas, trials, and heartbreak. There I am, usually in bed or on the floor, crying out to God, crushed by a new medical diagnosis for my child, a broken relationship, or severe, ongoing physical pain. I cry out, and he always hears me. He rescues me every time. I know you can relate—because we are all human, and suffering is part of life.

But today's verses fill me with hope. There are so many powerful promises packed into this passage. Psalm 34 as a whole is rich with God's assurances, so I encourage you to read the entire Psalm.

These promises are what you need when you feel stuck in the midst of trauma and heartbreak. You must remind yourself that God hears you, he delivers you from your troubles, and he is near to the brokenhearted and those crushed in spirit. It's also a reminder that you will face troubles.

Too often, people live with the false belief that they shouldn't go through hard things or endure multiple struggles in a row. But the Bible is clear that we will face troubles.

The more important reminder, however, is this: God will rescue you from them ALL. There is not one trial, struggle, or burden you are facing that he will not eventually deliver you from. That is truly hopeful and good news. You can rest in the assurance that God hears you, he will rescue you, and he will use it all for good. Oh, what a wonderful God we serve and love!

> ***PRAYER**: Father God, thank you so much for all the promises in your word. Thank you especially for the promises from today that you hear my cries and rescue me from all my troubles. Please help me to focus on you and trust those promises when I'm in the thick of suffering. In Jesus' name, amen.*

Reflection and Life Application

1) What verse from this section was most meaningful to me? *(Write it out here)* _____
_____
_____
_____
_____

2) What did I learn about having hope when life's hard that I didn't know before? Or what was I reminded of that I already knew? _____
_____
_____
_____
_____

3) What from this section on having hope when life's hard encouraged me and brought me hope?
_____
_____
_____
_____

4) How has my perspective on having hope when life's hard changed since reading through this section? _____
_____
_____
_____
_____

5) What will I do to maintain this new sense of hope when faced with suffering and trials? _____

_____
_____
_____
_____

6) Any other thoughts or takeaways about having hope when life's hard? _____

_____
_____
_____
_____
_____
_____

PRAYER: Heavenly Father, thank you for your promises and truths about having hope when life's hard. Please help me to take what you've shown me through this section on having hope when life's hard and apply it to my life. Help me remember that I can never be hopeless because Hope himself lives inside of me. In Jesus' name, amen.

ABOUT THE AUTHOR

Desiree Swift is a beacon of hope. As the Founder and Director of Eternal Hope Ministries, she is passionately dedicated to sharing the eternal love, hope, light, and truth of Jesus with those navigating their darkest moments. With a Master's Degree in Ministry and Practical Theology, and experience as a Community Chaplain, Desiree is more than just a Bible teacher—she's a spiritual warrior who inspires countless individuals through her sought-after speaking engagements, heartfelt teaching, and impactful writing.

As a mother navigating the challenging journey of childhood cancer, Desiree embodies "faith over fear." Despite her multi-year struggle with chronic pain from a broken back and other physical challenges, she shines with resilience and courage, reminding others that if she can persevere through her hardest moments, so can they. Desiree's life is a living testimony to the power of Jesus and the truth that with him, all things are possible.

Residing in Northern California with her amazing husband and two incredible teenagers, Desiree treasures her role as a homeschool mom, seeing motherhood as her greatest ministry. When she's not speaking, writing, or ministering to others, Desiree enjoys quality time with her family, reading captivating books, connecting with friends, and embracing the great outdoors.

AN INVITATION FROM THE AUTHOR

The most important relationship anyone can have is with Jesus Christ as their Lord and Savior. He is the reason I am able not just to survive the trials shared in this book, but to thrive through them. Jesus is my source of hope, truth, light, joy, peace, strength, and love. Without him, I am nothing, and I can do nothing.

If you feel a tug on your heart and desire a relationship with Jesus, I invite you to pray this simple prayer:

"Jesus, I believe you are the Son of God and you were crucified on a cross to save me from my sin and make me right with God. I admit I am a sinner and I am choosing to turn from my sin, selfishness, and any behavior that does not honor you. I choose you as my everything. I receive your forgiveness and ask you to take your rightful place to reign in my heart. Help me to become more like you and reflect you to the world with love, joy, peace, light, truth, and hope. Today begins a new life with you as my Lord, King, and Savior. Thank you for loving me and dying for me. In your mighty name, amen."

Once you've prayed this, I would love to celebrate with you! Email me at contact@desireeswift.com to let me know you've begun your relationship with Jesus. I also encourage you to connect with a local church to help you grow in your faith.

All funding from the sale of this devotional goes to inspiring hope and transforming lives with the love and truth of Jesus through Eternal Hope Ministries.

Made in the USA
Las Vegas, NV
22 March 2025